Many of us love, and strive to protect, wild rivers for the pleasure they give us—in contented contemplation of a river "because it is there" or in direct and intimate contact. But nobody expresses the kind of caring born of closeness better than Rod Nash does. To the histories, the myths, the anecdotes, the physical facts, and the inevitable concerns making up the body of river lore, he adds an element rare among authors: personal knowledge born of dealing with challenge. For Rod runs the Big Drops with style and exultation and, yes, love.

MARTIN LITTON, GRAND CANYON DORIES

This is armchair adventuring at its best. With a historian's perspective, an environmentalist's concern, and a boatman's know-how, Roderick Nash guides us skillfully through ten major rapids on several of the western rivers most beloved by recreationists. As with float trips themselves, the end comes all too soon, but when you close the book, you know you've had an unforgettable experience.

DAVID LAVENDER, AUTHOR OF RIVER RUNNERS OF THE GRAND CANYON

The big drops are center stage, the main attraction, on most of the rivers we run, and no one describes them better than Rod Nash. His eloquence captures both the excitement and fear all river runners feel poised on the brink of a watery precipice. And because he has been there, and has truly understood the experience of being there, he writes with rare insight about the power, both physical and spiritual, of moving water. Perhaps most importantly, Rod Nash brings the big drops, and the rivers creating them, to life as irreplaceable natural resources we can not afford to lose.

DAVID BOLLING, FRIENDS OF THE RIVER

River history and conservation are important ingredients and contributions to the enjoyment of rafting. To know the past is to be aware of the present—a copy of The Big Drops *should be in every river runner's personal library.*

DEE HOLLADAY, HOLIDAY RIVER EXPEDITIONS

In The Big Drops, *Rod Nash achieves a delightful blend of the historical and the present-day, and because he is first a river runner, he knows first-hand the emotions one feels when about to tackle high-gradient whitewater. If you have run any of these rapids, you must read this book to get a true appreciation of what you've accomplished.*

JACK NELSON, CASCADE OUTFITTERS

This is a book that makes a difference, one that sweeps the reader into the heart of whiteness and takes him on a wet-eared ride to Crystal-deep realizations that will remain long after the last page has been towelled off. The Big Drops can make a Big Difference, and fun had along the way is the same larger-than-life size.

RICHARD BANGS, SOBEK EXPEDITIONS

THE BIG DROPS

THE BIG

TEN LEGENDARY RAPIDS
OF THE AMERICAN WEST

REVISED EDITION

RODERICK FRAZIER NASH

Johnson Books: Boulder

To people who like their water white

Cover design by Molly Davis
Cover illustration by Molly Davis

LCCCN 89-63129

ISBN 1-55566-051-7

Printed in the United States of America by
Johnson Publishing Company
1880 South 57th Court
Boulder, Colorado 80301

CONTENTS

PUT-IN

"Put-ins" are where river trips, as well as books, begin. They are exciting places, hopeful places, nervous places. Put your boat on moving water and it's all downhill—except some of the hills are steeper than others. These are Big Drops: rapids, whitewater, places where rivers go wild.

Big Drops have been around as long as precipitation has fallen on land higher than the sea. You find them where the irresistible force of flowing water meets immovable objects: rocks. In the long run, of course, the river always wins. The moving water reduces the continents to sand and carries them to the ocean floor in preparation for the next continental uplift and the next generation of rapids. But for a time the hard rock resists, turning rivers into writhing white snakes. Put a boat on that stream of energy and motion and you are in for a big ride.

Moving water expends energy in the form of waves, but there are differences. In oceans and lakes the water remains stationary; the waves move. The opposite occurs on rivers. The waves stand still and the water moves through them. So, instead of being carried along on the face of a wave like a surfer, the river runner goes up and down as on a roller-coaster. To get an idea of the scale involved, think of yourself as sitting in a boat on the floor of your living room. The waves in Big Drops can be as high as the ceiling—of a room on the second story! Now think of being on the roof of that two-floor house and looking down twenty feet to the bottom of a dark, churning hole. Of course it's only water!

If river waves were smooth and regular, whitewater boating would be like an amusement park attraction—fun, a little scary, yet essentially predictable and safe. But the tons of water moving down a rapid every second have a nasty way of rising up and exploding unexpectedly in your face. There are reversals and whirlpools and surging eddy lines that can trap and hold boats and bodies for anxious seconds or minutes. Boatmen* talk about "the Maytag treatment" and "washing machines without walls." One thinks that running a big rapid is an experience comparable to that which a mouse has when it is flushed down a toilet! Now consider a generous assortment of exposed rocks randomly sprinkled down the rapid, add a border of logs and brush, include at times water so cold that it drains a swimmer's energy in seconds, and the full dimensions of the whitewater challenge become clearer.

So why do it? Why fool around with Big Drops? The answer is invariably subjective, but perhaps it is possible to do a little better than the mountain climbers' "because it is there." One starting point, at least for the Western rivers being considered in this book, is the pleasure of riding a magic carpet of moving water into some of the wildest country that remains in the contiguous United States. There is indescribable beauty here and a chance to reduce life to its essentials, to be truly self-reliant. Another factor is the satisfaction of being part of the most basic natural process: the washing of the earth back into the sea. Rivers are the blood of the rocks. Everything eventually ends up there—including river runners. People also float whitewater to find the challenge, indeed the fear, that our normally overcivilized lives occasionally crave. But if you are the kind of person who is paralyzed, rather than energized by fear, stay home and look at someone's slides. Boatmen seek to find in themselves that grace under pressure that Ernest Hemingway defined as courage. For many it is a religious experience absolutely necessary to their psychological welfare. Then there is the importance of being humbled by forces far stronger than themselves. Only the foolish, or the very novice, talk about "conquering" rapids; what you really conquer, if only for a moment, is your own insecurity. But that can be exhilarating, a peak experience. And so the boatmen come back, time and time again, to stand beside a wild river scouting a Big Drop.

---

*Here and throughout this book I will use this term without reference to sex. Especially in the last decade many women have become excellent "boatmen."

Rapids have a relentlessness about them that is unusual in the spectrum of outdoor recreation activities. There is no turning back, no reconsideration, no second chance. Commit a boat to the power of a Big Drop and you must make the run—in the boat or in the water, in one piece or several. By way of contrast, the mountain does not pull the climber upward at twenty-five miles per hour, demanding instant and irrevocable decisions. You can rappel off the cliff. You can also brake a sports car, fall down on the ice or off a surfboard, and luff a sailboat into the wind. But rapids do not grant incompletes. Only pilots, skydivers, and hang gliders, who also deal with gravity in a fluid medium, face a comparable everything-on-the-line finality. They know with the boatmen what Winston Churchill meant when he observed that if you "play for more than you can afford to lose, . . . you will learn the game."

Time was, and not all that long ago, when Big Drops were not run for fun and only rarely out of necessity. The explorers and pioneers, following the custom and often the trails of the Indians, routinely carried their boats around wild water. *Portage*, the French term for the laborious process, stuck. In more ways than one portaging was a drag, but for nearly three centuries in North America neither boats nor boatmanship were capable of handling major rapids. But there is a new clientele in the cowboy bars of places like Stanley, Idaho; Flagstaff, Arizona; and Green River, Utah. The new kids in town wear shorts and rubber sandals, but nobody snickers. The men and women who run rapids tend to be young, strong, cool under fire, and tanned the color of the rocks among which they work and play. Many of them have disdained careers in the established world in preference for a life on the river. They carry knives and pliers on their belts. They drink a lot of beer. When they talk, it is more often than not about Big Drops.

Defining a Big Drop is almost as difficult as running one. One person's terror is another's "piece of cake." Estimation depends on experience. Moreover, on a river, change is the only constant. Rocks shift position. Holes appear and disappear with variation in the flow. "Killer" logs appear and vanish overnight. It is quite correct that you never run the same water twice.

Knowing the choice of Big Drops would be controversial, I spent hours in the company of river friends guessing and second-guessing the rapids to include. Many were nominated. Snaggletooth on the Dolores River and Skull Rapid in Westwater Canyon of the upper Colorado had a number of advocates. Wyoming boaters mentioned high-water runs of Lunch Counter Rapid on the Snake as well as the presently-illegal descent of the Yellowstone River within the national park. California's Salmon River boasts a monster called Bloomer Falls which was even bigger before 1983 when the Department of Fish and Game blasted out some of its rock to facilitate fish migration. Staircase on the American's North Fork, Quartermile Rapid on the Merced, and Royal Flush on the lower Kern, all in California, are worthy nominees. Over on the eastern slope of the Continental Divide, boaters on the upper Arkansas fear Pine Creek Rapids.

Some say that entire reaches of Oregon's Illinois River, Idaho's Selway, New Mexico's Upper Taos Box section of the Rio Grande, and Cherry Creek section of the upper Tuolumne, or the Forks of the Kern run off the west side of California's Sierra are more difficult than anything treated in this book. I have run these rivers, and they have a point. But this whitewater has only been explored in the last decade. I preferred to discuss rapids that had more of a history, and I also leaned toward rivers more familiar to the average river runner. In fact I deliberately excluded truly awesome rapids that "hair" kayakers and helmeted paddle raft teams sometimes attempt. Niagara Falls, after all, has been "run" in a barrel! What I sought were rapids that are regularly run in rafts and dories, as well as kayaks, by commercially-guided, as well as private, groups. So the upper reaches of the Black Canyon of the Gunnison River below Crystal Dam is not included. It has spit out the shreds and splinters of the few kayaks that entered it. Indeed, boats that have passed through a canyon like this have made most of their progress on someone's shoulders! I was looking for rapids that could be *boated*. It may be, of course, that places like Dagger Falls on the Middle Fork of the Salmon, Selway Falls on the Selway, and Shoshone Rapid in Colorado's Glenwood Canyon will become routine runs of the future. But I suspect I will not be part of it.

On this point I mentioned in the first edition of *The Big Drops* (1978) that rivers like the North Fork of the Payette in Idaho would be left for bolder boatmen of the future whose equipment and technique may well surpass our own by a proportion equal to our distance from the nineteenth-century river explorers like John Wesley Powell. Two years later an article in *Outside* proudly announced that Nash's future was now: the North Fork Payette had been run in its entirety. But closer examination of the article suggested some qualifications. It seems that five kayakers started the descent, but only three finished—one after being knocked unconscious for a while. I still maintain that commercial rafting of this portion of the Payette is not presently feasible; it does not meet my criteria for a Big Drop.

While the present treatment is limited by design to rivers of the American West, the existence of formidable rapids in other parts of the nation should at least be acknowledged. The *Maid of the Mist* takes crowds of tourists on the Niagara River below the famous falls, but the gorge downstream contains huge and awesome hydraulics that only a few boaters have faced. The Chattooga River, shared by Georgia and South Carolina and made famous or infamous by the film *Deliverance,* has claimed over twenty lives in the last fifteen years. Most of these people were inadequately prepared and equipped (the river is frequently run successfully), but the fact remains that the Chattooga is a bigger killer than the Colorado in the Grand Canyon. West Virginia's New River has rapids such as Double Z and Greyhound Bus Stopper that are major league by any standard. So are Pillow Rock, Lost Paddle, and Iron Ring on the Gauley. Maine's Penobscot, New York's upper Hudson, and Pennsylvania's popular Youghiogheny (especially sections of the upper river like Tommy's Hole and Gap Falls) deserve consideration. It could be argued that the biggest eastern drop of them all is the Great Falls of the Potomac, almost within sight of the nation's capitol. A *Big Drops East* should be written by someone familiar with whitewater navigation in that part of the country.

And what about the "other" America: Alaska? Mt. McKinley's glaciers feed the mighty Susitna River that has turned back some of the nation's best kayakers. One descent of its major canyon was accomplished with the aid of a line from the boater to a helicopter hovering overhead! The Alsek River, which Alaska shares with British Columbia and the Yukon Territory, is so precipitous it thwarts migrating salmon. Walt Blackadar and a handful of kayakers have descended it when the river did not run under the tongue of a glacier for several miles!

There is also a worldwide dimension to whitewater boating, treated in part by Richard Bangs and Christian Kallens in their exciting book, *Rivergods,* and in *First Descents,* edited by Cameron O'Conner and John Lazenby. Bangs and most other international river runners honed their wildwater skills in the Grand Canyon of the Colorado. They have pushed on to river frontiers in Africa, descending the mighty Zambezi below Victoria Falls for the first time in 1981. Seven years earlier Ron and Marc Smith, also Grand Canyon veterans, helped a British expedition run the Zaire (formerly the Congo) through the Gates of Hell and the historic Stanley Falls. Canada lures the adventurous with the Grand Canyon of the Stikines, above Telegraph Creek in northwest British Columbia, which is so constricted in one place that the only exit from a rapid is under a submerged ledge! It's not a good place for an open boat. The most difficult river I have ever run is the Chilko through Lava Canyon in British Columbia. In 1987 it claimed six lives in two days! Papua New Guinea offers the Watut River, surprisingly large for an island until you remember it contains peaks over 15,000 feet in height. But there are bigger mountains in the world and they generate bigger rapids. The Andes in Chili are the source of the Bio-Bio where Richard Bangs and his Sobek outfit pioneered commercial boating in 1978. The Bio, says Sobek, makes the Grand Canyon's Lava Falls (see Chapter 10) look like a "cesspool," but funny thing, its first explorers named one of its crux rapids "Lava South." Further north along the Andes, the enormous Amazon has its source. I was turned back in 1979 by a sixty-foot waterfall on one of its tributaries, but Piotr Chmielinski, a Polish kayaker, has led the way down the Apurimac and also boated the Colca. The world's other major mountain massif, the Himalaya, powers incredible rivers on their way to salt water. On the south the tributaries of the Ganges and the Indus are beginning to be run. Boating down the northern slope of the Himalaya, through Tibet and China, has difficult political rapids to negotiate as well as the wet kind. The one American expedition that gained access to the Yangtze in 1986 did not complete the trip, but the river's astonishing Tiger Leap Gorge (theoretically narrow enough for a tiger to jump) has been floated by a Chinese adventurer inside a rubberized barrel. To date, the other great rivers that drain the northern Himalaya, the Mekong and Brahmaputra, have not been boated. It is good to know a few Big Drops remain to be run.

I undertook *The Big Drops* because I sensed that whitewater boating in the American West was entering a new era. The people who made early river running history are gone. No modern historian will ever have the opportunity of learning how it was at Lava Falls in the 1890s for George Flavell or Nathaniel Galloway. Now the second generation of western boatman, the organizers of the first commercial river running companies, for example, are passing from the scene. Much of their knowledge exists in perishable form—in warehouse and campfire talk. It was the right time, I thought, to gather and record this history before it, too, disappeared around the bend of time.

Along with the old timers, the old-time style of river running is vanishing before our eyes. Paved roads lead to many put-ins now, and there are mile-by-mile guidebooks for the rivers. Some of them even feature aerial photographs with lines showing the correct course to row or paddle. The opportunity to run rivers, once a function of skill and spirit, is now doled out by computer lotteries; and the waiting list, in the case of the Grand Canyon, is ten years long or, if you opt for a commercial trip, $1800 expensive. Running the Selway is a once-in-a-lifetime proposition—if you are lucky in the lottery. The number of people in your river party, where you camp, how you cook, and even the conditions under which you defecate are closely regulated. I have supported, indeed helped plan some of these rules. As river running became popular, they were necessities. But it is nonetheless sad to see the old, lonely, uncontrolled era—when wild rivers were synonymous with freedom—slipping away.

The other main reason for *The Big Drops* is to dramatize that, for all their power, rapids are highly vulnerable. Dam builders eye whitewater with as much enthusiasm as boatmen. Stored behind concrete, the energy that propels a boat can turn a turbine. In the arid West, dams are both agent and symbol of the civilizing process. In reasonable numbers they enhance our lives, but the balance is hard to maintain. A major portion of the greatest whitewater in the West has gone the way of the buffalo and the Indian—exterminated or confined to reservations called reservoirs. There are fewer major rapids left in the Lower 48 than there are grizzly bears. Some of those that have literally gone under are noted in the Honor Roll at the conclusion of this book. Big Drops are in fact the rarest outdoor recreation resource, and there are those who would dam every river discussed in the following pages. Instead, they deserve our best preservation efforts. I say reverse the present procedure: put *all* America's wild and scenic rivers in a protected category and require a specific act of Congress to remove them for development. And why not consider removing a few dams? We built them, and we can take them down. A relatively small structure like the O'Shaugnessy Dam on the Tuolumne in Hetch Hetchy Valley would be a good place to warm up for big demolition jobs like that involving Glen Canyon Dam. Hayduke Lives!

Future generations must know the joy of riding moving water in other places than amusement parks and roadside "wet and wild" slides constructed of plastic tubes. Technically difficult as they may be, the artificial whitewater racing courses—like the

$3.2 million one in South Bend, Indiana—do not compensate for the real thing. So it is gratifying to work in this book with a publisher, Johnson Books, which endorses river conservation in the strongest terms. It is also good to know that several dedicated organizations are presently working hard to ensure that whitewater boating has a future as well as a past. They include American Rivers, 801 Pennsylvania Ave. SE, Washington, DC, 10002; Friends of the River, Bldg. C, Fort Mason Center, San Francisco, CA 94123; River Defense Fund, 7600 E. Arapahoe Rd., Suite 113, Englewood, CO 80112; National Organization for River Sports, Box 6847, 314 N. 20th St., Colorado Springs, CO 80904; Sierra Club, 730 Polk St., San Francisco, CA 94109; and The Wilderness Society, 1901 Pennsylvania Ave, Washington, DC 20006. They deserve the support of all river runners.

The first edition of *The Big Drops* appeared in 1978 but in a very limited hardbound printing that has already entered the rare-book lists. I co-authored that book with Robert O. Collins whose skill as an historian and a writer is still reflected in this edition. I am grateful for the memories of thousands of river miles that we traveled together when the sport was still young. It is also a pleasure to pay tribute to my ancestor Simon Fraser (there was a spelling change on my side to "Frazier") and his son, Simon Roderick. In 1808 Fraser made a first descent to the Pacific Ocean of the British Columbia river that bears his name. His journal records the same anxiety and exultation that I experienced 150 years later when I began river running as a teenage guide on the Snake in Jackson Hole, Wyoming. In fact the only rapid I have ever portaged is one that my great, great, great grandfather and his Indian companions also carried around: Bridge River Rapids on the Fraser.

It is a pleasure to acknowledge for assistance in preparing this book veteran river runners such as Martin Litton, Fred and Maggie Eiseman, Georgie White, Jack Currey, P.T. Reilly, Kenny Ross, Ted and Don Hatch, Bryce Whitmore and the late Bill Belknap, Walt Blackadar, and Otis Marston. Others who have shared their knowledge and experience include Cort Conley,

Jim Campbell, Dick Barker, Bart Henderson, Bryce Whitmore, Ken Sleight, Don Neff, Ron Smith, Frog Stewart, William McGinnis, Wally Rist, Kim Crumbo, Joe Munroe, Vladimir Kovalik, John Blaustein, Richard Bangs, Frank Ewing, George Wendt, and David Lavender. Finally, I am grateful for the river friends without whom whitewater boating would have been lonely or impossible: Ron Hayes, Rick Smith, Ray Ford, Dee Holladay, Kenton Grua, Regan Dale, Tim Cooper, C. Ray Varley, Aron Friedman, John Hartman, Verne Huser, Melissa Berry, Sandy Nash, Honeydew Murray, Jennifer Nash Robertson, MaryAnne Nash, and Laura Nash Schwanauer.

Go with the flow!

RODERICK FRAZIER NASH   NOVEMBER 1987
                                         SANTA BARBARA, CALIFORNIA

It is difficult to find in life any event which so effectually condenses intense nervous sensation into the shortest possible space as does the work of shooting, or running, an immense rapid. There is no toil, no heartbreaking labor about it, but as much coolness, dexterity, and skill as man can throw into the work of hand, eye, and head—knowledge of when to strike, and how to do it, knowledge of water and rock, of the one hundred combinations which rock and water can assume—for these two things, rock and water, taken in the abstract, fail as completely to convey any idea of their fierce embracings in the throes of a rapid as the fires burning quietly in a drawing-room fireplace fails to convey the idea of a house wrapped and sheeted in flames.

SIR GEORGE BACK

Clavey
Falls

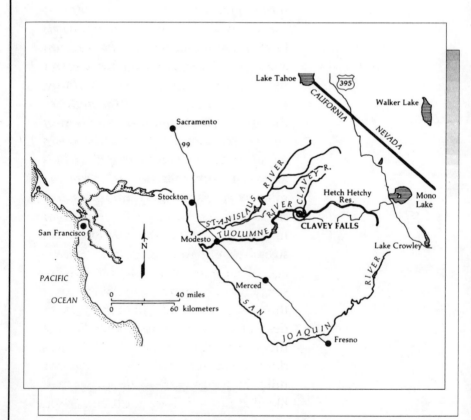

Lake Tahoe

395

Walker Lake

CALIFORNIA

NEVADA

Sacramento

99

ST-ANISLAUS RIVER

CLAVEY R.

RIVER CLAVEY

Hetch Hetchy
Res.

Mono
Lake

Stockton

San Francisco

N

TUOLUMNE

CLAVEY FALLS

Modesto

Lake Crowley

PACIFIC

OCEAN

Merced

SAN

RIVER

0   40 miles

0   60 kilometers

JOAQUIN

Fresno

Chapter 1

A long with large rocks, gravel bars, and resistant bedrock formations, a river's rate of descent creates Big Drops. The slope of a stream is usually measured in feet per mile, and some comparisons are useful in putting the Tuolumne (pronounced to-OL-uh-mee) River and Clavey Falls into perspective.

A mature river like the Mississippi lumbers from St. Louis to New Orleans at a rate of descent of about two feet per mile—just enough to keep Old Man River rolling along. The Colorado is a much younger, hence steeper, watercourse. Through the Grand Canyon of Arizona it drops 2,167 feet in 279 miles, an average of just under eight feet per mile. Water flowing down this kind of slope produces an alternating pattern of major rapids followed by mile-long calm stretches. Oregon's Rogue River averages 12.4 feet per mile, and its rapids are steeper and more frequent than those of the Grand Canyon. A still sharper rate of descent is found on the Middle Fork of the Salmon River in Idaho, which races downstream at an average of 27 feet per mile. In high water conditions, a river like this, or the Selway, just to the north, seems like one continuous rapid.

Then there is the Tuolumne. Pounding down a deep canyon through the golden foothills of California's Sierra Nevada, the section from Lumsden Camp to Wards Ferry drops 54 feet per mile, or seven times the rate of the Colorado in the Grand Canyon and twice the rate of the Middle Fork. Particularly during high water, many boatmen regard the Tuolumne as among the most challenging raftable rivers in the West. It is a relentless force, with rapids blending one into the other; only occasionally can a boatman escape the grip of the current to catch his breath and shake out his arms and hands. Then, as he looks back upstream, the Tuolumne appears to be a white staircase descending the Sierra.

The unusual name of this unusual river has its origins in the local Indian dialect. *Talmalamne* meant a cluster of stone wigwams. Given the multipurpose functions of most aboriginal words, *talmalamne* may well have referred to the circle of tipi-shaped granite peaks that form the main crest of the Sierra at the Tuolumne's source. Mount Lyell, 13,114 feet, is one such pointed landmark. The meltwater of two small glaciers clinging to its northwestern face starts the river.

In the next phase of its 158-mile length, the Tuolumne lives in high country, flowing through forested valleys that spread out at 8,600 feet into the largest upland meadow in the Sierra. A paved road brings thousands of visitors to Tuolumne Meadows every summer. Below this point, however, the river is seldom seen as it enters Muir Gorge and rages along the bed of a deep, precipitous canyon. A century ago John Muir scrambled through here, the din of falling water pounding in his ears. No one boats the Tuolumne at this elevation.

At 3,800 feet—still in Yosemite National Park—the river dies for a time in the greatest mistake in national park history. In 1913, after a protracted controversy, Congress authorized a dam at the lower end of Hetch Hetchy Valley inside Yosemite National Park. Completed ten years later, it created a granite-walled reservoir in a place once considered the aesthetic equal of Yosemite Valley, a few miles to the south. Many people today believe the Tuolumne ends in the Hetch Hetchy impoundment, its water diverted into aqueducts and destined for power plants, irrigation ditches, and the pipes and faucets of San Francisco. Some of the Tuolumne does, of course, go this route, but enough water remains in the river below Hetch Hetchy to make possible one of the West's most exciting whitewater rides. Indeed, to give the dam builders their due, the released water from hydroelectric operations has the beneficial effect of making the Tuolumne runnable in California's dry summer months.

A few miles below the Hetch Hetchy spillways, the Tuolumne can be run by experts in kayaks and modified, self-bailing rafts. This so-called Cherry Creek run has a gradient of between 80 and 150 feet per mile and is big time by anyone's standards. Below it, at Lumsden Camp, the increasing amount of water and decreasing rate of descent usually permit the use of standard inflatable boats. Barring mishaps, it takes only two hours to run the five miles to Clavey Falls, but the Tuolumne can spoil the best laid plans. Regardless of their skill, first-time boatmen on the Tuolumne pay their initiation dues to the river in the form of broken oars, upsets, and torn boats. At low water flows there is simply no way to miss all the rocks—you just try to minimize the impacts. The United States Forest Service, which manages the river once it leaves Yosemite National Park, used to place its registration box not at the put-in, but after the first two rapids, on the theory that any boatman who reached the registration point in one piece was either good enough or lucky enough to have a reasonable chance of completing the run.

The Tuolumne moves so quickly and drops so precipitously around so many blind corners that boatmen require several runs to decipher its obstacle course. The rapids present several possible channels and the need for an instant decision in very fast water. The wrong choice is quickly rewarded, and the unfortunate boatman is left draped around a rock, pinned on a log, or overturned at the base of an eight-foot waterfall. It is, of course, possible to walk down and scout the whitewater ahead, but how much river can one memorize? The Tuolumne's rapids are so long and complex that keeping a planned route in mind is extremely difficult. Once on the racing water, chosen landmarks or "cues" blur

into a pastiche of waves, rocks, and shoreline vegetation. Moreover, the Tuolumne is what boatmen call a "technical" river. It
demands a degree of precision in rowing and finesse in reading
and running fast water seldom required on the larger western
rivers. Trouble is commonplace on the Tuolumne. Those theo-
retical two hours to Clavey Falls can easily become two days, and
Clavey can put a permanent end to a river journey.

Just above Clavey Falls the Tuolumne relents a bit, as if to an-
ticipate its biggest drop. After threading slots only inches wider
than the raft and setting up to ride down a succession of sudden,
sharp ledges, it is a blessing to sit at the oars and look at the
scenery. Then ahead on the right appears a flash of whitewater
that first-timers mistake for Clavey Falls. It is, rather, the last few
yards of the Clavey River, blasting through boulders to make a
grand entrance into the Tuolumne.

The Clavey is a major tributary, with branches reaching sixty
river miles to the top of 9,000-foot ridges north of the Tuolumne's canyon. The name comes from an English immigrant,
William Clavey, whose widow and son tried to run cattle from the
1890s to the 1940s in the chaparral-choked foothills between the
Tuolumne and the river that bears their name. The Clavey fun-
nels water and, during storms, large rocks, down a very steep gradient along the north side of Jawbone Ridge. Tumbling into the
Tuolumne, these boulders make Clavey Falls. The Tuolumne
powers through them and smashes into a sheer, two-hundred-
foot cliff opposite the mouth of the Clavey River. The cliff re-
strains the river, forcing it into the boulders. The result is a long,
spectacular clash of an irresistible force against an immovable
object that leaves even the most seasoned boatmen stunned
when they see it for the first time.

Clavey Falls is divided into two main channels by a large island of boulders that clogs the middle of the Tuolumne. The
flow on the right side is larger, but leaps fifteen feet down a rock-
studded chute into a maelstrom of green and white. The vertical
drop of the left channel is only half that of the main falls on the
right, but a left-side run brings boats dangerously close to the
base of the cliff and its churning whirlpools. Below the boulder

island, the right and left channels converge just in time to plunge through a formidable hole, and twenty feet farther on, the current splits savagely around a large rock, the "alligator." Below this obstacle come two sharp drops in low water or a series of large standing waves in high, and finally a tight, rocky bend to the left. From the top of the main falls to the bend is almost a third of a mile.

The challenge of running Clavey Falls begins with the landing to scout the rapid. Because of the cliff, scouting must be done from the right shoreline, which also features the Clavey River confluence. Usually the Clavey is too fast and too deep to ford safely, so the only alternative is to remain in the boats until its mouth is passed and then pull to the right bank. The maneuver sounds easier than it is since only thirty feet separate the Clavey confluence and the start of the fast water at the top of Clavey Falls; moreover, the Clavey enters the Tuolumne with a force sufficient to kick a boat into the main current and propel it straight for the falls. With everyone intensely aware of the Big Drop just ahead, there can be momentary panic as the boatman power-strokes onto the little gravel beach just a few yards from the brink.

With bow lines tied and double-tied to brush or a boulder, it is time to go and look at Clavey Falls. Styles vary. Some boatmen dash down the shoreline, leaping rocks and splashing through small pools. They hurry to wait, unmoving, on the ledge below which the main falls thunder. Others try to play it cooler, perhaps joking with passengers, but soon they too stand silently on the ledge over the falls. By unspoken agreement boatmen at first say little in such situations. Their eyes move constantly, searching for routes. After a time someone will venture an opinion. It will be discussed, modified, and discussed again with much pointing and even stone-tossing in an effort to pinpoint a location in the rapid.

On a right-side run the first difficulty is the small rocks above the main falls. The boatman must pick his way through them carefully in order to reach the lip of the falls with his bow pointed straight down the only clear chute. Too far right and he will plunge into a churning white vortex that could hold an over-turned boat and its former passengers indefinitely. If he misses the chute in the other direction, the boat will hurtle over the lip of the falls to smash on the jumble of sharp, black rocks in the center of the river. The least serious mistake is to slip into the main chute sideways; the boat will simply capsize and its occupants swim the rest of Clavey Falls. Entered correctly, boats in the chute tilt sharply downward at angles approaching sixty degrees. Standing almost vertically on his foot brace, the boatman anticipates the jolt at the bottom on the fall. Two water-covered ledges flash by underneath; then dagger-sharp rocks appear to the left and right. Oars are useless at this point. Even if a boat propelled by such force could be controlled, the amount of air beaten into the water by the fall makes it futile to dig and pull a blade; you cannot pull against bubbles and foam. Accurate prior positioning is the only key to a successful passage through the top of Clavey.

The alternate way to run the first part of these falls is down the left-hand channel, to the left of the boulder island and close to the cliff. In low water this run is mandatory. It begins with a row across the Tuolumne; there is a little room on the left bank before the cliff to land and read the water. At first glance it appears impossible to get a boat through the jumble of table-size rocks with which this route through the rapid begins. The lesser of many evils seems to be a narrow, twisting passage about fifteen feet out from the shore. The current is fast here, and the boatman must pivot repeatedly to keep from jamming his raft against a rock. There is little room to maneuver. Broken oars are a distinct possibility, and to lose control in this way would be disastrous, since the twisting slot drops boats into a foaming pool just above the falls. There is only time for one, perhaps two, strokes, and they must accomplish two things: keep the boat off the cliff face and straighten it for the plunge over the fall. The frightening price of not making effective use of the moment in the pool is to have a boat pinned into a crevice in the cliff. Held as in a vise by the raging current, the boat fills with water and either capsizes or moves sluggishly sideways over the fall to a probable flip.

Once below this fall, the worst may seem to be over, but Clavey holds more surprises. One moment a boat is ten feet out from the cliff in five-foot waves and more or less in control, the next it is up against the rock wall. The explanation is the powerful current pouring down the right side of the rapid and intersecting the left-hand route at this point. Anything floating, such as a riverboat, goes along for an unwelcome ride headlong into the cliff. Only by anticipating the sideways blast, angling the boat, and rowing hard can boatmen avoid eating rock. It is no different for boats using the right channel. So great is their speed coming off the chute over the main falls that they are propelled straight across the Tuolumne and into the cliff.

Some boatmen try to fight the hydraulics and keep off the cliff. It is also possible to go with the flow and play the cliff as one would the side of a pool table, deliberately allowing the boat to ricochet and, according to the angle of rebound, making the necessary adjustments to ride through what is known as "the big hole in Clavey." A large rock, eight feet off the cliff, is the problem. In low water it is exposed, inviting boats to wrap around its upstream side; quick thinking and rowing are essential to dodge it on either side. Higher flows cover the rock, but create a monster hole. Most boatmen simply straighten out and slam into its center. They know their rubber boats will fold into a "V," but they count on the speed of the current to spit them out on the downstream side. The best position, if you can get there, is right of center where a ribbon of water carries up and over the big wave.

All that now remains of Clavey Falls is the long, alligator-shaped rock with a sharp upstream edge that can slice rubber like a razor, and another hundred yards of waves and ledges. Invariably a boat is so heavy with water at this point that control is difficult. With a final effort the boatman pulls to the right and attempts to land in the fast water along the steep right bank. Many fail in this endeavor and are obliged to run several hundred more yards through another, very rocky rapid before they can relax.

Within a half day's drive of fifteen million people, it is remarkable that the Tuolumne was not run until the 1960s. The

first known attempt was that of a group of fishermen from Sacramento who thought it would be easier to float the river than walk
along its banks. They were in for a big surprise. By the time they
reached Clavey Falls, both boats and morale were in tatters, and
they wisely portaged the Big Drop. Their report, and that of the
few hikers who reached the bottom of the Tuolumne's canyon,
discouraged river runners until 1965, when Knoel Debord, a
Sierra Club member from Oakland, took a kayak down the river.
Debord portaged Clavey, as did Gerald Meral and Richard Sunderland on November 4, 1968, when they kayaked the Tuolumne. Meral and Sunderland did, however, exercise the privi-
lege of pioneers and name several pools and rapids. Excited by
what they had seen in the canyon, the men returned the following May and, with Jim Morehouse, kayaked the river. Its flow was
4,800 cubic feet per second—ideal for an attempt at the right
channel in Clavey Falls—but unfamiliarity bred conservatism,
and again they carried their boats around the rapid. The first
known kayak run of Clavey occurred on July 20, 1969, at a flow
of 4,000 cubic feet per second. Sierra Club boaters, including a
fourteen-year-old girl named India Fleming, made the run without incident.

The summer of 1969 also marked the beginning of rafting
on the Tuolumne. Bryce Whitmore, a veteran California river
outfitter, had been searching for an alternative to the Stanislaus
River for his commercial trips. He wanted a longer, more challenging journey on a less crowded river. Whitmore and a team of
his best boatmen tested the Tuolumne for a week in late July and
found the flat, self-bailing "Huck Finn" rafts they used quite capable of handling the river. At Clavey, however, they carried the
rafts down the right shoreline. The next season Whitmore scheduled several trips on the Tuolumne, but his brochure carried the
warning that the river "requires the best equipment, most skilled
oarsmen, and lightly loaded rafts." The run, he added, was "not
recommended for your first whitewater trip, or for the faint
hearted." But, he concluded, the Tuolumne offered more thrills
and more challenge than any eighteen river miles in the American West. Few who made the run with Whitmore disagreed, even

though they continued to portage their boats around Clavey Falls.

In May 1970 Bob Collins and I brought our rafts to the Tuolumne. Bryce Whitmore told us the run would take lots of time, and that was an understatement. We spent hours crashing through thickets of manzanita and poison oak along the river to study its rapids, but we still had trouble. One of our boats ripped open on a rock, lost air, and wallowed helplessly down a quarter mile of rock-strewn waves. Another wrapped around a rock, filled with several tons of water, and had to be extricated with fixed ropes from shore. Running scared by the time we reached Clavey Falls, we landed well above on the right and barely managed to stumble across the torrent coming down the Clavey River. The sight of the rapid left us limp; there seemed no way it could be run. We paced the right shoreline again and again, staring at the white fury.

Today's perspective is different, but since no one had yet put a raft through this Big Drop, we could not be sure if a boat would make it down the falls, between the rocks, and through the big hole. At length we decided to portage and walked back to where the boats were tied. But our minds continued to churn, and as we reached the boats we turned to look back downstream to where the Tuolumne vanished into the space above Clavey Falls. "Why not?" we thought simultaneously. After all, we had come to run, not walk, the Tuolumne, and it was precisely challenges like this that brought us to wild rivers in the first place.

Once we were committed, the run went smoothly enough. It was unnerving above the falls, slaloming through random rocks, aiming for a chute we saw only in our memories. At what seemed like the last possible second, it opened ahead of us. For a moment we hung poised on the brink. Then, unbelievable speed. The rocks we had studied from shore for so long went past in a blur. Ahead was the cliff: we leaned on the ten-foot oars, not really rowing but straining, in a kind of isometric exercise, against a constant force. Even so, one boat glanced off the rock wall. The beauty of inflatables is that they bounce rather than shatter or dent, and this time we won the billiard game between rubber and rock. Rebounding off the cliff, the raft spun into perfect position for the big hole. It seemed much larger on the river than it had from the shore, but there was that thread of water moving through the reversing wave. We adjusted to hit it square on; then, with Grand Canyon instincts, pushed with the oars to increase the raft's momentum going into the hole, thus giving it a better chance of popping through. It did, but knee-deep with water, and there was no time and no one to bail. We struggled to keep our unwieldy boats facing downstream as we plowed over and through the lower waves and ledges. In one sense the weight was a blessing—a boat carrying an extra ton of water has a low center of gravity and is very hard to flip. In landing such a heavy boat, however, you pay the price. Only after several abortive attempts could we make the raft stick into a semblance of an eddy along the shore, leap out, take a turn with the bow line around a rock, and notice our hands shake as we tied up.

In time others came to try their hands at Clavey Falls. Some got through and some did not, but everyone learned this was a "technical" as opposed to an "equipment" rapid. The distinction is clear and important. On big water, such as the Grand Canyon's Lava Falls, the equipment brings you through. A big boat compensates for the boatman's mistakes; it may get pounded, but it will generally float out the downstream end right side up. It is almost (but not quite) impossible to flip one of the giant pontoons. These big rigs are usually run straight down the middle of a rapid. They eat every hole, yet they flush out. Try the same technique on the Tuolumne, and your trip, if not your life, will end in the first mile. The Tuolumne is a "technical" river because expertise in reading whitewater and rowing it precisely is mandatory for a successful run. A mile on the Tuolumne calls for more maneuvering than a hundred miles on the Colorado. But with Sierra snowfields melting down the Tuolumne in May and June it is sometimes the case that neither big boats nor skilled boatmen ensure a safe passage.

One June a few years ago, a group of campers near the Tuolumne put-in were startled by the sudden appearance at their evening fire of a boatman who worked for a leading western river outfitter. He seemed shaken, but after several cups of coffee began the story of his day at Clavey Falls. Because of the high water, his company had cancelled its scheduled trip and bused the would-be passengers out of the canyon. The boatmen, however, decided to run for their own fun. There were two boats: a rowed raft carrying two men and a stripped-down boat that five persons attempted to steer with canoe paddles. With many of the Tuolumne's rocks covered by the high water, they shot down to Clavey Falls in an hour. No one had ever attempted the Big Drop with so much water in the river, careening down the main falls and somehow negotiating the quarter mile of ten-foot waves beyond. The paddled raft ran second, with the boatman at the campfire among its crew. He was washed over the side below the main falls and recalled nothing but an occasional gasp for air until he was pulled from the river by the rowers at the end of the rapid. The three men waited and waited, peering upstream for a sight of the paddled raft and the four remaining members of the group. Nothing appeared, and, fearing the worst, they ran up the right shoreline. Still no raft. Then they saw it, pinned into an eddy against the cliff and trapped so securely that the four remaining paddlers were helpless in their efforts to work back into the downstream flow. The possibility of their swamping and drowning in that whirlpool was desperately evident. The cliff prevented any rescue from river level, so the three on the right shoreline ran back to their boat, crossed the Tuolumne in calmer water below Clavey, and climbed the back side of the cliff with a long rope and some rock-climbing hardware known as Jumar ascenders. Locating a big ponderosa pine on the top of the cliff directly over the beleaguered boat, the rescuers tied on and lowered their rope. One by one the people on the river climbed the line a hundred vertical feet to safety. The last task was to pull the empty raft straight up the cliff and carry it below Clavey Falls.

Whitewater boating had barely begun on the Tuolumne when it seemed destined to end. On December 4, 1968, the San Francisco Public Utilities Commission released a report proposing more intensive use of the river's "remaining power drop" for

hydroelectric generation. A new dam below the one already re-
straining the river at Hetch Hetchy Valley was proposed, along
with a series of tunnels and a generating plant right at Clavey
Falls. Actually this was repetition, not innovation. In 1907 the
Tuolumne Electric Company erected a hand-fitted stone powerhouse a mile below Clavey. It supplied electricity to rim commu-
nities until 1938, when a giant storm put 38,000 cubic feet per
second in the Tuolumne and cleaned out all but the foundations
of the bridge and building.

Initially San Francisco's 1968 proposal did not elicit much
opposition. Few knew what was at stake, but the Sierra Club, remembering Hetch Hetchy like the Alamo, was instinctively suspi-
cious of the city's plans for the river. Rather than build new
dams, the Club argued that the existing ones on the Tuolumne
should be removed. As Michael McCloskey explained, "We've already had the experience of reclaiming logged-over land for
parks. We think it's time the same concept be applied to dams."
By the early 1970s McCloskey, along with many environmentally
conscious Americans, was asking quite seriously if dams added to
or detracted from the quality of a society's life. In a state that had
intensively utilized its flowing water and, in the case of the Stanislaus River, was about to eliminate its most popular whitewater
run, a wild Tuolumne was an especially precious resource. The
United States Congress, at least, held this view. On January 3,
1975, it designated the Tuolumne a "study" river for the National
Wild and Scenic Rivers System. This action placed a moratorium
on further development and mandated public hearings. The
Turlock and Modesto Irrigation Districts, San Francisco water interests, and hydropower companies were the leading advocates
of further development on the Tuolumne. In 1983 they spent
$140,000 a month in lobbying efforts. On the other side, Friends
of the River and the Tuolumne River Preservation Trust led one
of the most vigorous campaigns in American river protection history. The turning point came when actor Richard Chamberlain,
who had run the river and fallen under its spell, joined the fight,
declaring "we have the power to destroy [the Tuolumne], but
never, never in our wildest imagination can we ever recreate it."

Victory came on September 28, 1984, when the Tuolumne was added to the National Wild and Scenic River System. River people everywhere were delighted, but many understood that given the realities of trade-off politics, the price of saving the Tuolumne was the life of the now-dammed Stanislaus.

And then, incredibly, in the summer of 1987 Donald Hodel, Secretary of the Interior in the Reagan administration and successor to the notorious James Watt, proposed the *removal* of O'Shaugnessy Dam in Hetch Hetchy Valley. The upper Tuolumne would resume existence as a wild river and a "second Yosemite Valley" would be recovered for the national park. Except for hydropower, what would be lost? The water that San Francisco and the irrigators covet would still come down the river and could be removed further downstream—closer, in fact, to the fields and the city by the bay. River people were uncertain whether Hodel's suggestion was a political ploy or a serious effort to right an historic wrong. But the Secretary went to Hetch Hetchy and smilingly posed holding an Earth First! T-shirt featuring Edward Abbey's dam-destroying "monkeywrench" symbol. Miracles may yet occur.

Meanwhile, Clavey Falls continues to generate improbable stories. One evening Bryce Whitmore camped several miles below it on the big beach opposite Indian Creek. As the rafts were being unloaded, it became painfully clear that the box of cooking pots was missing. To his chagrin Whitmore remembered leaving it in his garage at home. Lacking the means even to boil water for coffee, the party scoured the bushes for rusted pots prospectors might have abandoned, or any container that would hold water. As dusk fell, Whitmore saw a box floating down the middle of the Tuolumne. Someone rowed out and brought it into camp. To the astonishment of the hungry campers, it contained a complete set of pots and pans. There was no explanation, except prayers, for its presence until several other packs and bags appeared in the river. Then an overturned raft floated past. Whitmore towed it to shore but found no sign of its former occupants. By this time it was dark and dinner was simmering in the newly acquired pots; then out of the darkness came a shout from upstream, and into the circle of firelight staggered four disheveled river runners. They told how they had flipped in the big hole in Clavey that afternoon. Their boat had continued on downstream too fast to follow on foot through the Tuolumne's dense riparian vegetation, so there was no alternative but to walk on down the river in the hope of finding the boat caught in an eddy. Just as they were about to give up the search and climb out of the canyon, they saw the light of Whitmore's fire through the trees. Dinner, served from their own pots, never tasted better.

The boatmen sometimes refer to the major rapids as Christian Falls. Why? Because they make a believer out of you.
EDWARD ABBEY

Rainie
Falls

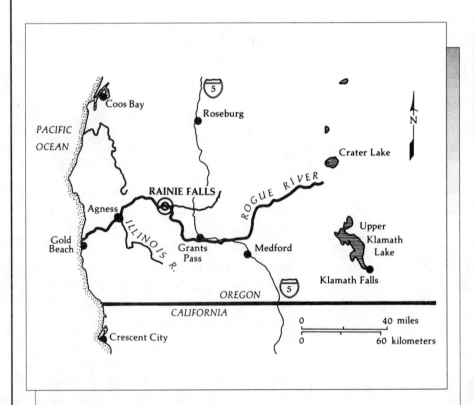

Coos Bay

Roseburg

PACIFIC
OCEAN

Crater Lake

RAINIE FALLS

ROGUE RIVER

Agness

ILLINOIS R.

Upper
Klamath
Lake

Gold
Beach

Grants
Pass

Medford

Klamath Falls

OREGON

CALIFORNIA

N

Crescent City

0   40 miles
0   60 kilometers

Chapter 2

You are on your way to run the Rogue. Depending on where you started, you may be driving west through the hot, treeless Great Basin of the western states. As the open miles of Utah and Nevada slide by, and the temperature soars into the hundreds, it is tempting to fantasize about green canyons and clear, cool water.

Think of the Rogue and you think of western red cedar, Douglas fir, Port Orford cedar, western hemlock, sugar pine. On the ocean side of the coast ranges, fog and rain create a lush vegetation and a junglelike understory—myrtle, rhododendron, azalea, dogwood, dense skeins of wild grape, and an astonishing variety of ferns.

You also think about wildlife. No one who has run the Rogue forgets the sight of a great blue heron, poised in the shallows, still as stone. When the boats come too near, the bird vaults upward and cruises the spaces between the shoreline pines with slow, powerful wingbeats. Often there is ocean-born fog on the lower river. Through it deer move like wraiths. At night, on your ground cloth, you can hear their hooves as they graze near your camp. The Roosevelt elk are more wary, preferring the high ridges. But

black bears prowl the river banks; you see their tracks on Solitude Bar, and at night they crash through the brush, annoyed at
the intruders on their favorite beaches. Float quietly, look carefully, and your chances are good for seeing the best river folk of
them all—the otters. They are totally at home in water, and their
frolicking always brings admiring smiles to less skillful river travelers. Mergansers streak up and down the river corridor; king-
fishers dart across it to snatch a fly; and high overhead the osprey
and the eagle circle imperiously, eyeing the blue thread set in
the green velvet. Such images make the searing miles of a
Nevada summer seem shorter.

Oregon's Rogue River is born at 5,200 feet in the Cascade
Range near the ancient exploded volcano that now contains
Crater Lake. It starts as a small mountain stream, then drops into
the broad, fertile Rogue River Valley, where the farms and or-
chards around Medford and Grants Pass are usually clouded by
haze from lumber mills. The Rogue moves on, searching for the
Pacific. The Klamath and Siskiyou mountains stand in its way,
and over the ages the river has cut a canyon. The best scenery
and whitewater are here. There are no roads. People refer to this
stretch of the river as the "wild Rogue."

The Rogue has been called "the fishingest river in the West."
In summer it is too warm for much action, but as the weather
gets worse the salmon and steelhead fishing improves. You can
stand at a major rapid like Rainie Falls and watch one of the
greatest shows in the West. At unpredictable intervals a great
fish, fighting the current to return to the place of its birth,
throws its twenty, thirty, or forty pounds into the air. Arching
over the tumbling water, tail lashing for added momentum, the
fish tries to climb a wall of water. Few make it up the main falls of
Rainie; the rest fall back into the white cauldron at its base. Later
they find easier going up side channels and continue on their
ancient mission of self-perpetuation.

Rich in fish, game, and timber, the watershed of the Rogue
inevitably became a bone of human contention. The Indians,
Takelmas, were the first claimants, but the Europeans who began
to trickle into southwestern Oregon in the late 1830s called

them simply the Rogues. Isolated in the canyon, they had little contact with the coastal Indians and none with the early explorers and fur traders. They had lived from a time beyond memory in this lovely land of fish and animals and flowing water. They hunted deer, elk, otter, and beaver, but most of all they derived their sustenance from the river. They would wait patiently on the ledge below Rainie Falls to spear the salmon and steelhead rising in the pool below.

The trappers were the first white men to venture into the canyon of the Rogue. Peter Skene Ogden led a party of Hudson's Bay Company trappers into the area in March 1827. Others followed. Michel La Framboise brought his brigade of trappers into the Rogue River Valley in 1833. But the trapper presence was fragmentary, and in just over a decade settlers were following their footprints. They wanted land for farms, not river canyons, and for them the Rogue River Valley was a place to pass through. Langford W. Hastings, in his *Emigrants' Guide to Oregon and California*, described the Rogue in 1845: "Its current is very rapid, and it has numerous falls and rapids, which obstruct its navigation, even for boats and canoes." Modern day river runners would agree.

Relations between the Indian and the white newcomers were hostile from the beginning and remained so until the Rogues were finally forced from the river country. As early as 1834 the Rogues were attacking the settlers passing between the Willamette Valley and California. Every year thereafter they assaulted the wagon trains, provoking increasing hostility on the part of the Oregon settlers. The settlers, though, were going through to more fertile land and learned not to linger and retaliate. Not so the miners who came out of California in 1851 and spilled over the Siskiyou Range and down into the Rogue River Valley. Unlike the farmers, the miners were a tough, brawling, barbarous lot, prepared to fight anyone for their claims, and quick to rally against any and all who might oppose them. Unhindered by law, order, or any authority other than their own greed, they killed indiscriminately and without remorse. They began with the Rogues.

From 1851 until June 1856 the Indians and the miners, known as volunteer companies, fought viciously. The prize was the Rogue River. Harassment, pitched battles, and treachery characterized the relations between the miners and the Indians. In the autumn of 1855 the volunteer companies, supported by federal troops, launched the final campaign against the Indians. The Rogues fought back against miners and troopers first at Galice, where today many river trips begin. The Indians retired to Grave Creek, a mile and a half above Rainie Falls. The volunteers and troops pursued; they were driven back on the high ridge above Grave, but rallied and followed the Indians into the depths of Whiskey Creek, a mile below Rainie Falls. Here they could not dislodge the Rogues, and the campaign was abandoned. The Rogues were left alone to winter by Rainie Falls, but their respite from fighting was only temporary. In the spring of 1856 the volunteers and federal troops again took the field, and at Big Meadows on the Rogue, the Rogues fought their last battle. On June 10, 1856, they left for the Siletz Reservation at the headwaters of the Willamette.

Silence settled over the Rogue River Canyon. The human drama had reached its conclusion, and today, driving over the Nevada desert toward the river, one might think of those tragic days. But they were not without adventure, and adventure, after all, is still sought in our own turbulent times. And so, in the shimmering heat of the desert, the mind wanders to the Rogue's ultimate test—running Rainie Falls.

For boatmen the upper river poses few problems. Children from families camped in the roadside park dabble about the river on inner tubes and air mattresses. Where the road ends at Grave Creek, the river becomes more serious. The whitewater below the bridge is the first major rapid; its deceptive boulders have broken many oars, punctured many tubes, and caused not a few river parties to question the wisdom of attempting the trip. It is always sad to see dreams die, but Grave Creek Rapids is a well-placed filter. Better to wipe out here, where cars are within walking distance, than to abort a trip deep in the roadless canyons ahead.

There are other memorable rapids on the Rogue. In low water Tyee Rapids demands a run that literally kisses the grassy right bank. Wildcat offers two routes around an island at the entrance, then options end as boaters must pick their way down a rock-studded chute. The pieces of broken boats decorating it are incentive enough to make the right moves. Black Bar Falls is a succession of sudden, four-foot drops—no problem for larger boats taking them bow first, but that position is easier to visualize than to attain in the complex currents of a narrow gorge.

Most boatmen who don't run Rainie Falls regard Blossom Bar as the most demanding rapid on the river. The first problem is to locate the rapid. It is easy to float on calm water past the huge rocks at the entrance and suddenly find it necessary to row for your life. Wiser boatmen climb the cliff on the right and scout the river as it tears through a "rock garden" the length of a football field. A successful run involves at least three total reversals in direction: right, left, right, and sometimes left again. It is necessary to pull hard each time, stop the boat, spin it, and pull hard back again. Timing is the key, and only the very best oarsmen avoid a "billiard shot" off one of Blossom's many rocks. There were more of them before the 1930s, when Glen Wooldridge, who first ran and portaged the river in 1915, used explosives to blast a wider channel for his boats. His technique was interesting. He rowed up the rocks at the head of Blossom, lit a special water-resistant fuse connected to a charge of dynamite, dumped the charge overboard and rowed quickly downstream before the blast.

Mule Creek Canyon lingers in the mind after a run down the Rogue. It is more a tunnel than a rapid in the usual sense, and the adventure begins when the Rogue, normally 50 to 100 feet wide, cuts a narrow trench into bedrock. Narrow, in this case, means *narrow;* most of Mule Creek Canyon is only ten to fifteen feet wide. At the Coffee Pot, an aptly named, bubbling, circular chamber in the rock, the whole Rogue River moves through an eight-foot passageway in solid rock. Turn a seventeen-foot raft sideways, and you stay awhile. Fortunately there are no ledges or midstream rocks in Mule Creek Canyon, but it is always a sobering experience to enter the mouth of the longest, narrowest passage of any major river in the West. Near the end of the chasm there is a reward. Look quickly to the left and spot a graceful waterfall, bordered by ferns, dropping in several stages over the canyon wall into the Rogue.

And there is Rainie Falls, the Big Drop of the Rogue. Even the name is difficult. It originated as a memorial of sorts to a nineteenth-century prospector and fish gaffer named Reamy or Ramey, who was killed by Indians in the vicinity of the falls. But Reamy soon became Rainy or, as the United States Forest Service standardized it, Rainie. The mist that perpetually hangs over the drop may well have inspired the change.

Rainie is more of a pure waterfall than any of the other Big Drops. There are no rocks to dodge, no intricate route to follow. In one clean, quick leap the Rogue plunges fifteen vertical feet over a ledge. At the bottom is a frightening spectacle: a chaos of white, churning water that on first glance appears destined to swallow and hold any boat exposed to it. And that's all there is to Rainie. Below the drop the Rogue quickly regains its composure. Rainie is both the shortest and, potentially, the most dangerous of the Big Drops.

The river above the falls is as calm as the river below. There is plenty of time to hear the booming thunder, note the mist rising in the air, and see the Rogue drop out of sight. Boatmen land on the left, tying to small trees whose bark has been worn smooth over the years by the bow lines of river travelers. A long ledge of rock running parallel to the river affords an excellent vantage. Rainie is also the Big Drop to which you can get the closest; the falls drops away virtually beneath your feet.

At Rainie Falls you understand the situation as soon as you walk up to inspect the run, for it lacks the sophistication of other Big Drops. The river plummets smoothly over the lip and down the face of the ledge. So far, so good. But then the Rogue goes crazy. Technically, what happens is a reversal. The water dropping over the falls plunges to the bottom of the river channel, and, deflected upward out of this hole, mounds into a back-curling wave six to eight feet high. So strong is this down-up-and-around motion of the water that the topmost levels of the hole actually flow strongly upstream. A boat, log, or body going over the falls is first driven down almost vertically near the bottom of the riverbed. The next motion is sharply up on the curler wave and on downstream—perhaps. The alternative, and always a very real possibility in Rainie, is to remain in the hole between the falls itself and the reversing wave. A boat would eventually be spit out, but nothing that breathes oxygen could be expected to survive more than a minute or two.

The prospect of being trapped by the current at the base of the falls is uppermost in the mind of the boatman standing on the rocks at the lip of Rainie. He studies the water, repeatedly allowing his eyes to follow a single patch of water over the falls and into the hole. His hope is to find a ribbon of water that consistently moves through the reversal and might therefore carry his boat along with it. But the complex hydraulics below a drop like Rainie are difficult to follow. At a given moment there is an order of sorts to the shape and direction of the boiling waves, and the same order will reappear in an irregular cycle. In between, other things are happening. The inescapable conclusion is that a successful run in a drop like this depends in good part on chance. There is no way of calculating what the moving water will be doing the moment your boat is passing over, through, and under it. Catch the cycle at one phase, and you can pop through with astonishing ease. A second or two later, in exactly the same place, you may be going against the grain with the river hammering and tearing at your boat and body. It is that element of unpredictability that causes boatmen to stand and stare at Rainie Falls for long, anxious minutes.

There are several approaches to the curved lip of the falls. The far right drops onto exposed rocks—no way! The far left has the advantage of a secondary buffer wave reflecting off a rock. Riding it down lessens the jolt at the bottom but exposes boats to the danger of a sideways or quartering attitude, and the big reversal makes quick work of boats that do not hit it square, bow to stern. The center route offers a better chance of taking the reversal directly on the bow, but the drop is very steep. A boatman

running center discovers that instead of sitting down he is standing, feet braced against the rowing frame in front of him. The
crunching jolt at the bottom folds the rubber boat around him.
Should he fail to brace solidly, knees slightly bent like a skier ab-
sorbing the shock of a mogul, he will almost surely be pitched
over the bow of the boat into the raging water at the base of the
falls.

These realities give Rainie its reputation. They explain why it
has a rating of VI on the international scale of whitewater difficulty: "Very dangerous. Limits of possibility. Many who inadver-
tently or unwittingly try this level do not survive. Experts generally leave it alone!"

In truth, many choose not to run Rainie. There are several
narrow channels skirting the main falls on the right. Salmon use
the fish ladders on the far right to avoid the big ledge, and river
runners can walk their boats down its series of pools. Or, closer
to the falls, they can bump and grind larger inflatables over a
succession of lesser ledges.

Until recently almost every river traveler on the Rogue bypassed Rainie Falls in this way. The wooden "drift boats," ances-
tors of the modern whitewater dories, that Glen Wooldridge began using on the Rogue in 1915 had excellent maneuverability,
but were not really designed for big waves and extreme turbulence. Wooden boats, moreover, usually came out second best in
collisions with rocks such as those that line the channel immediately below Rainie Falls. So a tradition of *not* running Rainie developed among the local Oregon guides. It was said (and even
printed on the official river map) that a portage around Rainie
was "mandatory." Some even implied it was illegal to run the
falls.

This state of affairs existed with regard to the biggest rapid
on the Rogue when Zane Grey arrived in Grants Pass, Oregon,
on September 3, 1925. Grey was a fishing fanatic, and his best-
selling westerns financed his passion. The Rogue soon became
his favorite trout and salmon stream and the setting for his novel
about commercial *versus* sport fishermen: *Rogue River Feud.* He
built a substantial cabin at Winkle Bar and visited it regularly for

the fall fish runs until his death in 1939. Grey had much to say
about the early attitude toward Rainie Falls. On his initial 1925
trip down the river he used four eighteen-foot skiffs, canoe-
shaped craft with a narrow, blunt stern, sharp bow, and high
gunwales. Each had two seats and watertight compartments at either end. There were also four twenty-three-foot dories in his
party. Zane Grey did things in the grand manner.

The Zane Grey party put in below the hamlet of Galice and
experienced their first problems at Grave Creek Rapids, where
jagged rocks tore open one of the skiffs. It sank immediately, a
lesson not lost on later designers of multichambered inflatable
rafts. Undaunted, Grey's party pressed on to Rainie Falls. None
of his guides even considered running the rapid. They landed
on the right on rocks that, according to Grey's journal, were "almost impossible to stand upon." Grey also recorded that all the
luggage in the seven remaining boats had to be carried 300 yards
around Rainie Falls. The group toiled for hours. Then it was
time to bring the boats around. Grey described the process:

"My boat was the fifth in line to go down the chute. I waded
down the rocky channel, holding hard. There was no one to
help at the moment, and I imagined that I could do it alone.
When my heavy boat turned into that pitway it shot down like a
flash. I could not hold the rope. My feet were jerked from under
me and went aloft, while the back of my neck, my shoulder and
right elbow crashed down on the rock. I was almost knocked out.
Fortunately, the boat lodged below and soon the men got to it. I
had all I could do for the time being to drag myself out of the
water to a safe place. I thought my arm was broken but, fortunately, I had sustained only severe bruises. My heavy shoes were
studded with hobnails, yet were as slippery on those infernal
rocks as if they had been ice."

At extreme high water, to be sure, Rainie fills in, becoming
just a succession of rolling waves. Veteran Oregon guide Bob
Pruitt ran it under such conditions in a wooden drift boat.
People were stranded by the flood downstream, and Pruitt went
to the rescue. He left Hellsgate at the improbable time of 2:00
A.M. and reached Agness, forty miles downstream, in seven

hours. With the Rogue racing along at twenty miles per hour, Pruitt had little choice but to run Rainie Falls. There was virtually no chance to get to shore once his wild ride began.

Glen Wooldridge also has a highwater story. In December 1955 a huge storm raised the Rogue twenty vertical feet. Fred Hale, a local pilot, attempted to take supplies to one of the roadless lodges along the river but lost his way in the thick clouds and "landed" on a mountain side. When the plane did not report, Wooldridge and his son launched their twenty-foot, flat-bottomed boat and screamed away down river on the strength of a twenty horsepower outboard motor. They hardly slowed for Rainie Falls and found the pilot, badly injured, a few miles below. Loading him onto a cot in the bottom of the boat, they tried to continue, but the big velocity waves pounded their boat so hard that the unfortunate Hale landed in the bilge in eight inches of water. Finally they made it to a lodge where the pilot was rescued by helicopter.

At lower water levels no one attempted Rainie in a hard-hulled boat. But in the 1960s a new generation of boatmen with new kinds of boats came to the canyons of the Rogue. Schooled in the heavy water of the Colorado and the sharp drops of the foothill streams of California's Sierra, the newcomers looked at Rainie less as an impossibility than as a supreme challenge. Their inflatable boats bent rather than shattered on impact and bounced back for more. In the event of a flip, an inflatable could serve as a giant life preserver to which people could cling. The state of the art in whitewater boating was also improving, and river runners were trying and achieving feats that left old-timers incredulous. It was tempting, standing above Rainie Falls, to "go for it." The rocky portage, as Zane Grey had reported, was laborious, time-consuming, and in terms of injury to legs and ankles, probably just as dangerous as the main falls. But the compelling consideration for river runners, as for climbers of ice and rock walls, was the challenge. Like Everest, Rainie Falls was there. Could it be run?

Obviously there was risk involved, but river runners, like climbers, live with risk; it is what brings them to Big Drops in the first place. "Will I be safe on your trip?" customers frequently ask whitewater guides. "Absolutely not," one invariably replies. Then, with a twinkle in his eye, he adds, "If you want to be totally safe, stay in bed—alone!"

Thus it came to pass that what was insanity for one generation of boatmen became a reasonable risk for another. Rainie Falls began to be run. Usually most of the passengers and essential equipment are unloaded first. Life preservers have a special value in such situations, and they are carefully adjusted and tightened. The run is scouted; the "cues" for the entry memorized. Back in the raft, inevitably, second thoughts arise: Should I go for it? Is it crazy to jeopardize boat, gear, and the success of the river trip for one exhilarating moment? Why am I here anyway? What is life?

Exerting the usual damming effect of a Big Drop, Rainie slows the Rogue; boats move at a snail's pace as they approach the lip of the falls. The boatmen stand on their seats and look ahead, though there is not much to see except space and spray and the river moving on into the distance. The three-foot entrance waves require some attention. Finally it is too late for reconsideration. The boat gathers speed, tilts down and farther down. On good runs it is over in a flash: the shuddering jolt, the darkness of the big hole, the bow straining to climb the reversal wave, the tailwaves below: ten seconds at most.

Then there are the other kinds of runs. The boat slams down and does not climb up. Caught between the falls and the reversal, the boat veers sideways. It is very dark, very wet. The boat overturns, leaving its passengers to the mercy of the river. One involuntary swimmer at the base of Rainie traveled underwater down the Rogue for three hundred feet before surfacing unconscious but alive. He was wearing a good life preserver, too. A large dog without a preserver also dumped below the falls and was never seen again, despite hours spent pacing both shorelines. Still, many sane, successful runs of Rainie Falls have been made. The water level, the quality of the equipment, and the skill of the boatman are all determining factors. Given adequate assurance on these counts, the odds tilt in your favor.

With so many Big Drops in the American West either drowned in reservoirs or threatened with inundation, it is encouraging to know that in October 1968 Congress placed an 84-mile section of the Rogue in the National Wild and Scenic Rivers System. With a history of recreational boating as long as that of any other western river, the Rogue was an obvious nominee for the first group of eight rivers to be protected under the new legislation.

The National Wild and Scenic Rivers Act established three categories of protection, depending on the degree of development of the river corridor. The system applies nicely to the Rogue. From the Applegate River's confluence with the Rogue to the bridge at Grave Creek, the Rogue is a "recreational river." This means that there is abundant road access and considerable shoreline development. The objective of management (in this case the Bureau of Land Management and the United States Forest Service) is to control further development and maintain the river in a free-flowing condition—no dams or irrigation works. The thirty-three miles of river below Grave Creek, including Rainie Falls, are in the category of "wild river." Here management is instructed by the act to maintain wilderness conditions (no roads or further development) and to encourage primitive types of recreation. Unfortunately, from some perspectives, several lodges and the use of power boats continue on parts of the "wild river" section of the Rogue, permitted because they existed prior to 1968—"grandfathered in." Below the roadless canyon, the Rogue again becomes a "recreational river" and, for a few miles, a "scenic river," which means that some road access and construction exist.

Management of the Rogue has recognized that this river has exceptional appeal to noncommercial or private boating parties, many of them just beginning to master whitewater skills. With the exception of Rainie Falls, which all beginners would do well to portage, there is no reason why a serious group of novices cannot float the river safely. Given the existing roads and backcountry lodges, assistance is never more than a few hours away. Consequently, nonguided, do-it-yourself use of the Rogue has been vigorously defended. Some private boaters like John Garren have risked fine and imprisonment to make their case for equitable access to the river. And management, acting in the face of opposition from some guides and commercial river running companies, has generally defended a fair opportunity for the self-outfitted use of the river. The present annual breakdown is 42% commercial and 58% noncommercial.

The days you run Big Drops, like Rainie Falls, make for great camps. The tension of the run mellows into satisfaction. Zane Grey caught the mood of the Rogue after Rainie. He had camped, as modern runners often do, on the big beach at Whiskey Creek. And his party, like today's, drank up the beauty and perhaps some of the creek's namesake. Grey wrote about "idyllic days . . . dream days . . . warm drowsy days in which it seemed always afternoon."

Looking back at Rainie from below, Grey also had an appropriate idea for the use of Rainie Falls. "It'd be a good idea for the government to put their criminals in boats and send them down the Rogue to shoot the falls. If any of them got to Gold Beach (where the river enters the Pacific Ocean) alive, they'd deserve to be set free."

Hell's Half Mile

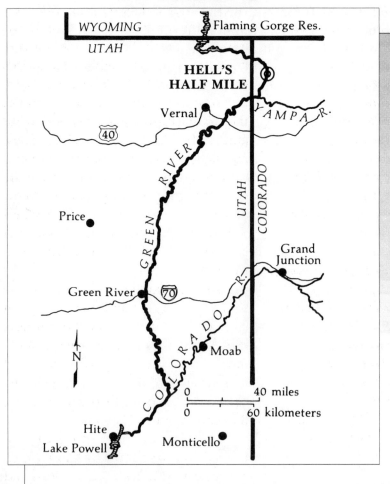

WYOMING — Flaming Gorge Res.

UTAH

HELL'S HALF MILE

Vernal

40

YAMPA R.

GREEN RIVER

Price

UTAH COLORADO

Green River

70

COLORADO R.

Grand Junction

COLORADO R.

Moab

N

0   40 miles

0   60 kilometers

Hite
Lake Powell

Monticello

Chapter 3

At one place as we were being hurled along at a tremendous speed we suddenly perceived immediately ahead of us in such a position that we could not avoid dashing into it, a fearful commotion of the waters, indicating many large rocks near the surface. The Major stood on the middle deck, his life-preserver in place . . . and peered into the approaching maelstrom. It looked to him like the end for us and he exclaimed calmly, "By God, boys, we're gone!"

FREDERICK S. DELLENBAUGH

The sun of the Colorado-Utah borderland is bright at noon, and the sky between the rock walls of the Canyon of Lodore is a dazzling, rich blue. The boatmen pull their rafts slowly out of the current and nose into the left bank. Someone ties the bow line to a tree. Everyone hears the sounds of the river—the gurgle of eddies swirling around the rocks along the shore, the call of a canyon wren, the swish of air among the water reeds and box elders, and behind these intermittent sounds a continuous low thunder from where the river disappears downstream in a flurry of spray. The boatmen hear that sound with their guts because they know what it means. With deliberation they weave through the rocks and disappear into the trees toward the portage trail. Here, trudging along a path worn dusty by a century of river travelers, the sunshine broken by pine and juniper, it seems unnaturally quiet. They top a low and rocky ridge and the roar is in their ears again. Occasionally, through the trees, they can see Hell's Half Mile.

The Canyon of Lodore on the Green River was named by Andrew Hall, a Scotsman who made his way West and at only nineteen became a crewman on

John Wesley Powell's great expedition down the Colorado River in 1869. Hall was shot down in 1882 while guarding a stagecoach and is now forgotten and unknown except for that moment when he looked at the dramatic portals of the Canyon of Lodore and remembered the nursery rhyme "The Cataract of Lodore," written in 1820 by the English poet Robert Southey. The poem is about moving water and the way it goes:

Rising and leaping,
Sinking and creeping,
Swelling and sweeping,
Flying and flinging,
Writhing and ringing,
Eddying and whisking,
Spouting and frisking,
Turning and twisting,
Around and around
With endless rebound!
Smiting and fighting,
A sight to delight in;
Confounding, astounding,
Dizzying and deafening the ear—with its sound.

Andy Hall also knew the last line of the poem, "And this way the water comes down at Lodore." So the canyon was called Lodore despite the protestations of the American frontiersmen with Powell who disliked anything European.

No one forgets the entrance to Lodore Canyon, Powell's "gates of Lodore," where the Green River enters the Uinta Mountains of northeastern Utah. The Uintas are one of the few major mountain ranges in North America that extend east to west, rising as a great dam through which the Green River has cut its path. Some twenty-five million years ago the watershed of the upper Green River drained eastward into the North Platte and ultimately to the great basins of the Missouri and Mississippi, cutting along the way the valley now called Brown's Park. From the crest of the Uintas the lower Green drained south and west

into the basin of the Colorado. Then twelve to fifteen million
years ago the eastern end of the Uinta Mountains dropped 4,000
feet, forming a large trough. At the same time the present Continental Divide rose in the east. Blocked from flowing eastward to
the Platte, the Green River formed a chain of lakes in Brown's
Park and eventually penetrated southward through the Uintas.
Then the Uintas began to rise, and simultaneously a warmer,
postglacial climate produced large amounts of water. The two
parts of the ancestral Green River joined. One major stream now
flowed southward out of Wyoming to gouge Lodore, the deeper
canyons to the south and west, and, ultimately, to join the Colorado in southeast Utah.

Humans have been passing through Brown's Park, just upstream from the Gates of Lodore, for centuries. The Indians and
the mountain men came to Brown's Park and moved on. Today
campers arrive in their recreational vehicles only to depart. Even
boatmen do not linger but pull downriver across the sagebrush
flats to the hard rock of Lodore. The ominous Gates of Lodore
dominate the southern end of Brown's Park with cliffs rising two
thousand feet, dwarfing the cottonwoods of the park. In Brown's
Park there are mosquitoes, saw grass, and mud; in Lodore, rock
and moving water. All of the early adventurers entered the Gates
with foreboding—and rightly so. In May 1825 the famous en-
trepreneur of the fur trade, William Henry Ashley, passed
through them to Hell's Half Mile with deep premonitions of
disaster.

> As we passed along between these massy walls, which in a great
> degree exclude from us the rays of heaven . . . I was forcibly
> struck with the gloom which spread over the countenances of
> my men; they seemed to anticipate (and not far distant, too) a
> dreadful termination of our voyage, and I must confess that I
> partook in some degree of what I supposed to be their feelings,
> for things around us truly had an awful appearance.

Ashley was born in Virginia in 1778. Looking to the west like
his fellow Virginians Lewis and Clark, he went to the Missouri

Territory when he was thirty years old. There he prospered, mining saltpeter, and met Andrew Henry, who mined lead near Potosi in southwest Missouri. As the demand for lead and saltpeter declined after the war of 1812, they looked for new financial opportunities. Ashley was an extraordinary man. Active in the territorial militia, he advanced from captain in 1813 to general in 1822; the following year he was elected lieutenant governor of the new state of Missouri.

Politics prospered no more than mining, however. In 1824 Ashley was defeated in the election for governor of Missouri and, like many losers, went west. As early as 1822 he and Andrew Henry sought their fortunes in the reviving fur trade. They dramatically altered the conduct of the business: instead of trading with the Indians for pelts, Ashley brought men west to trap the beaver. Trapping demanded different talents than trading, and Ashley found men who combined these skills. They were a new breed—the "mountain men." Spreading out through the rivers and canyons of the West, the mountain men trapped so well that the beaver nearly became extinct. At the end of summer they gathered at a rendezvous to sell their pelts. This institution, too, was Ashley's doing. Instead of establishing a series of fixed trading posts similar to those constructed throughout the West by Hudson's Bay Company, Ashley held a yearly rendezvous at crossroads like Brown's Park where the trappers could bring the pelts to trade for the goods of eastern America.

On April 21, 1825, Ashley launched his bullboat on the Green River, known then by the Crow Indian name of Seeds-ke-cee. Floating through Red Gorge to leave his name at Ashley Falls, he emerged on Tuesday, May 5, 1825, into Brown's Park. The Indians enjoyed this open, level valley along the Green and so did the mountain men. After Ashley's exploration, they frequently made it the site of their annual fur-trading rendezvous. It was a French Canadian, Baptiste Brown, who wandered into the basin, built himself a cabin, managed the rendezvous, and put another name on the map of the West. Brown's Park was a land of big sky where in the late summer the trappers and Indians bartered their pelts, drank whiskey, fought, fornicated, and prepared for the coming winter in the lonely canyons which stretch through the forests of the Uintas to the Colorado Plateau. Ashley brought the men to the mountains, but he was not one of them—a Jim Bridger or a Jedidiah Smith or a Jim Beckwourth. He returned west only once, in 1826. In that summer he sold out to a company of young men who were later famous in the lore of the West—Jedidiah Smith, David E. Jackson, and William L. Sublette. Ashley himself returned to Missouri, was elected to Congress, and continued a successful political career in Washington. What remained of Ashley's voyage was a message carved into the rocks of Flaming Gorge—"Ashley 1825"—and his journal, which describes how he and his men portaged around the rapids of Lodore to make their way down to the confluence with the Yampa, Whirlpool and Split Mountain Canyons.

After Ashley came William Manly, a hardy Vermonter who started west as a twenty-nine-year-old roustabout, got the gold fever, and headed for California. When the leader of Manly's wagon train announced in Wyoming that he intended to spend the winter of 1849 in Salt Lake City, Manly and six companions looked at the clear, placid Green River as a quicker pathway to the gold fields. Their first boat, an abandoned barge, did not survive Ashley Falls. Continuing in two twenty-five-foot dugout canoes, Manly and his friends "found generally more boulders than water" in the rapids of Lodore Canyon. It may have been in Hell's Half Mile that one of the canoes swamped, and several of its occupants nearly drowned. That was enough for Manly. He abandoned the river route in the Uinta Basin and proceeded overland, ultimately reaching California after a harrowing trek across Death Valley.

Ashley and Manly lost no boats in the Canyon of Lodore, but over forty years later John Wesley Powell was not so fortunate. The first major rapid in Lodore, which he named Disaster Falls, destroyed the *No Name*, a twenty-one-foot craft made of oak planking with watertight compartments. Its boatman, O.G. Howland, carried Seneca Howland, his younger brother, and Frank Goodman, an Englishman, along for the ride. Powell described the misfortune of June 9, 1869 in considerable detail:

I walk along the bank to examine the ground, leaving one of my men with a flag to guide the other boats to the landing place, I soon see one of the boats make shore all right and feel no more concern; but a minute after I hear a shout. Looking around I see one of the boats shooting down the center of the sag. It is the *No Name* with Captain Howland, his brother, and Goodman. I feel that its going over is inevitable and run to save the third boat. A minute more and she turns the point and heads for shore. Then I turn downstream again and scramble along to look for the boat that has gone over. The first fall was not great, only 10 or 12 feet, and we often run such. Below the river tumbles down again for 40 or 50 feet in a channel filled with dangerous rocks that break the waves into whirlpools or beat them into foam. I pass around a great crag just in time to see the boat strike a rock and rebounding from the shock careen and fill the open compartment with water. Two of the men lost their oars, she swings around, and is carried down at a rapid rate broadside on for a few yards and strikes amidships on another rock with great force, is broken quite in two, and the men are thrown into the river, the larger part of the boat floating buoyantly. They soon seize it and down the river they drift past the rocks for a few hundred yards to a second rapid filled with huge boulders where the boat strikes again and is dashed to pieces and the men and gradments are soon carried beyond my sight. Running along I turn a bend and see a man's head above the water and washed about in a whirlpool below a great rock.

The swimmers eventually crawled out of the river on the midstream island below Upper Disaster Falls. Jack Sumner rescued them in one of the expedition's two remaining boats. But the loss of food and equipment dogged the party for the remainder of its run. Powell blamed O.G. Howland for the disaster that named the rapid, and the festering of that relationship may have contributed to Howland's decision over a month later to leave the trip at Separation Canyon in lower Grand Canyon. He and his two companions were never seen alive again.

Today boatmen do not regard the scene of Powell's 1869 mishap as the crux run in Lodore. They hit the slots in Upper

Disaster, skirt the island and snake through the rocks of Lower
Disaster and Triplet to squat in the dirt of the portage trail, surveying the currents and rocks of Hell's Half Mile. A golden rabbit bush is in full summer bloom, but few notice it. All eyes—
tired, experienced, fearful, and sometimes wise—read the rapid
and its thirty-foot drop. The tumultuous water, jutting boulders
and long rock garden make Hell's one of the most difficult
rapids on the rivers of the American West.

The boatmen move down through the cedars and pines to
the rocks below. Here they do not find the grandeur of the
Grand Canyon, the lush greenery of the Salmon, or the bright
quartzite of Cataract Canyon. Their gaze is held by a maze of
huge boulders through which they must find a way. No stream
has deposited these house-size rocks; they fell a long time ago
from the canyon walls. Between the rocks and over them and
around them the Green River swirls. What does the boatman
see? What does he feel as the sun beats down on the dusty trail
by the raging rapid? This rock is exposed; that one is covered.
It's easier on the right. Certain trouble down the left. Usually
they are somber and serious, but sometimes cavalier. The thunder from water meeting rock continues. When faced with the
river in all its power, boatmen sometimes concentrate on the insignificant and the trivial; they may turn away from the river to
examine an evening primrose. Then, by unspoken signal, the
boatmen suddenly stand erect and trudge back along the
portage trail, slosh through a shallow stream, and work their way
down through a stand of juniper to the start of Hell's Half Mile.

Powell did not scout the rapid very long on June 15, 1869;
one look was enough. His journal records the moment:

During the afternoon, Dunn and Howland, having returned
from their climb, we run down, three-quarters of a mile, on
quiet water, and land at the head of another fall. On examination, we find that there is an abrupt plunge of a few feet, and
then the river tumbles, for half a mile, with a descent of a hundred feet, in a channel beset with great numbers of huge boulders. This stretch of the river is named Hell's Half Mile. The re-

maining portion of the day is occupied in making a trail among the rocks to the foot of the rapid.

Then, on June 16, the work began:

Our first work this morning is to carry our cargoes to the foot of the falls. Then we commence letting down the boats. We take two of them down in safety, but not without great difficulty; for, where such a vast body of water, rolling down an inclined plane, is broken into eddies and cross currents by rocks projecting from the cliffs and piles of boulders in the channel, it requires excessive labor and much care to prevent their being dashed against the rocks or breaking away. Sometimes we are compelled to hold the boat against a rock, above a chute, until a second line, attached to the stern, is carried to some point below, and when all is ready, the first line is detached, and the boat given to the current, when she shoots down, and the men below swing her into some eddy.

At such a place, we are letting down the last boat, and, as she is set free, a wave turns her broadside down the stream. . . . They haul on the line to bring the boat in, but the power of the current, striking obliquely against her, shoots her into the middle of the river. The men have their hands burned with the friction of the passing line; the boat breaks away, and speeds, with great velocity, down the stream.

The *Maid of the Canyon* is lost, so it seems; but she drifts some distance, and swings into an eddy, in which she spins about until we arrive with the small boat and rescue her.

Hell's Half Mile was actually named by John F. Steward on Powell's second expedition down the Colorado in 1871. Frederick S. Dellenbaugh's record of this trip is the most accurate and readable account of early river running on the Colorado. He was only seventeen when he left Green River, Wyoming, with Powell on May 22, 1871. Dellenbaugh secured his place through a relative, Almon H. Thompson, who was Powell's brother-in-law and second-in-command of the expedition. Fortunately, Dellenbaugh had talent as well as connections. He painted the first pictures of the canyon country, and in later years tramped all over the world, recorded his travels, and helped to found the Explorers Club.

On June 23, 1871, Dellenbaugh recounted in his journal the rigors of lining Hell's Half Mile:

> The entire river for more than half a mile was one sheet of white foam. There was not a quiet spot in the whole distance, and the water plunged and pounded in its fierce descent and sent up a deafening roar. The only way one could be heard was to yell with full lung power. Landing at the head of it easily we there unloaded the *Dean* and let her down by line for some distance. In the worst place she capsized but was not damaged. Then the water, near the shore we were on, though turbulent in the extreme became so shallow on account of the great width of the rapid here that when we had again loaded the *Dean* there were places where we were forced to walk alongside and lift her over rocks, but several men at the same time always had a strong hold on the shore end of the line. In this way we got her down as far as was practicable by that method. At this point the river changed. The water became more concentrated and consequently deeper. It was necessary to unload the boat again and work her on down with a couple of men in her and the rest holding the line on shore as we had done above. When the roughest part was past in this manner, we made her fast and proceeded to carry her cargo down to this spot which took some time. It was there put on board again and the hatches firmly secured. The boat was held firmly behind a huge sheltering rock and when all was ready her crew took their places. With the Major clinging to the middle cabin, as his chair had been left above and would be carried down later, we shoved out into the swift current, here free from rocks. She literally bounded over the waves that formed the end of the descent, to clear water where we landed on a snug little beach and made the boat secure for the night. Picking our way along shore back to the head of the rapid, camp was made there as the darkness was falling and nothing could be done that night.

The work began again the next morning:

All hands were up early and the other two boats were taken laboriously down in the same manner as the *Dean* had been engineered, but though we toiled steadily it was one o'clock by the time we succeeded in placing them alongside that boat. Anticipating this, Andy's utensils were taken down on the *Nell*, and while we were working with the *Cañonita*, our good chef prepared the dinner and we stopped long enough to fortify ourselves with it. Having to build a train in some places in order to carry the goods across ridges and boulders, it was not alone the work on lowering the boats which delayed us. While we were absorbed in these operations the campfire of the morning in some way spread unperceived into the thick sage-brush and cedars which covered the point, and we vacated the place none too soon, for the flames were leaping high, and by the time we had finished our dinner at the foot of the rapid, the point we had so recently left was a horrible furnace. The fire was jumping and playing amidst dense smoke which rolled a mighty column, a thousand feet it seemed to me above the top of the canyon; that is over 3000 feet into the tranquil air.

Some of those who followed Powell down the Green left indistinct trails. In 1891 a man named Snyder upset in Lodore, borrowed a horse and road over the mountains. We know nothing more. George F. Flavell ran a flat-bottomed skiff through Lodore in 1896 with Ramon Montos, but, like Powell, he lined Hell's Half Mile. There were probably others. Man's curiosity is unquenchable, and a flowing river irresistible. But river men tend not to be very literary, and many of these early pioneers were not even literate.

Julius F. Stone, however, was different. Stone came to Lodore in 1909 because of Nathaniel T. Galloway, but the men were remarkably dissimilar. Stone was a wealthy industrialist and investor from Columbus, Ohio; Galloway a semi-literate hunter and trapper from Vernal, Utah. They met because of a mutual interest in Robert Brewster Stanton's gold mining operation on the Colorado at Lee's Ferry. In his quiet and unassuming way Galloway was a genius. Since the 1880s he had wandered through the canyons of the Colorado Plateau trapping and hunting. Stone thought that Galloway had the most astonishing knowledge of animals and their ways of any man he had ever known. He was, in a sense, the last of the mountain men.

But Galloway's genius went beyond trapping beaver and shooting deer. Before him, boatmen rowed down rivers as they would on a placid lake. The bow of the boat was pointed downstream, and one or more oarsmen would pull hard with their backs to the waves and holes and rocks. With their backs to the rapid the boatmen theoretically had the strength and power to move the boat faster than the river, so that the speed would be sufficient to control the boat by a rudder guided by another man. Dellenbaugh graphically described this way to run rapids, rightly pointing out, however, that it was unnerving to the oarsmen to enter a dangerous rapid with their backs to the rocks and waves, relying on rowing faster than the current to maintain maneuverability.

"Than" Galloway changed all this in the early 1890s. Instead of rowing blindly backwards into a rapid, Galloway turned his boats around, faced downstream, and rowed against the current. This simple but astounding difference marked the beginning of modern river running, and to this day the technique is used by every boatman on the river. Not only can a boatman enter the rapid looking downstream to see where he must maneuver to avoid the rocks and holes, but he dramatically increases his maneuverability by pulling backward and across the current, using the "ferry" angle, moving from one side of the river to the other, picking his way downstream. Moreover, by pulling upstream against the current there was no need to have a separate steersman in the stern, for the oarsman could now slalom through the rocks and holes and eddies. Orders no longer had to be shouted back and forth above the roar of the torrent.

Galloway's first well-known river trip occurred in 1895 when he traveled alone from Green River, Wyoming, to the confluence and then up the Colorado to Moab. In September 1896 Galloway started down the Green River from Henry's Fork, coming upon Frank Leland and William Chesley Richmond at Little Hole. Intrigued by the prospect of adventure in the deep canyons to the south, Richmond agreed to accompany Galloway, and in February 1897 they completed the river run to Needles, California. We do not know if Galloway lined Hell's Half Mile on this trip.

By this time rivers were in Galloway's blood, and he was making profits from trapping the beaver which inhabited them. Later in 1897 he trapped and hunted down the Green River from Vernal, Utah, to Lee's Ferry, where he packed out westward through the pines of the Kaibab Plateau. From then on, each year found Galloway on the rivers. Always inquisitive, he experimented with new boats including one made of steel which survived the run from Green River, Wyoming, to Green River, Utah, through the Canyon of Lodore and Hell's Half Mile. Perhaps by then his experience was sufficient to run the rapids rather than line his boats. About this time he convinced Julius F. Stone it was feasible to boat the Green and Colorado through the great walls of time. In the autumn of 1909 he led Stone into the canyons.

This was the first whitewater trip in the West that could be termed "commercial," in the sense that a sportsman seeking recreation hired a guide. Stone was an avid outdoorsman and had considerable experience on Canadian rivers. He had talked to John Wesley Powell before that explorer's death in 1902. But Stone did not follow Powell's advice to use heavy oak boats that could withstand collisions with rocks. With Galloway he built light, maneuverable crafts. The idea was to *miss* rocks. Made of five-eighths-inch Michigan white pine, the Galloway-Stone boats were sixteen feet four inches long, four feet wide, and sixteen inches deep. They were flat-bottomed, weighed 243 pounds, and were intended for only one man. There were watertight compartments in each boat and a canvas shield to keep the cockpit dry from splashing water.

With Galloway in the lead, the Stone party negotiated Ashley Falls and in four days passed into the Canyon of Lodore. Much to Stone's dismay, Galloway insisted on running all the boats down the most dangerous rapids himself after the equipment had been unloaded and portaged around the rocks. So he snaked the boats through Hell's Half Mile while the others walked, stumbling over the boulders and slipping in the slime, along the remains of the portage path which Powell and his men had built many years before.

Two years later, in 1911, Ellsworth and Emery Kolb used Galloway-designed boats to travel downriver from Green River, Wyoming, to the Gulf of Mexico. Like Powell, the Kolb brothers carried their equipment around Hell's Half Mile. Floundering over the limestone boulders, they tumbled down through gullies where scraggly cedars tore their clothing. The Kolbs spent the whole day carrying their loads around Hell's Half Mile and then slowly lined their boats down through the lower rocks:

> With a short rope fastened to the iron bar or handhold on the stern, this end was lifted on to the crosspiece, the bow sticking into the water at a sharp angle. The short rope was tied to the stump so we would not lose what we had gained. The longer rope from the bow was thrown over the roots of the tree above and we both pulled on the rope until finally the bow was on a level with the stern. She was pulled forward, the ropes were loosened, and the boat rested on the crosspieces. The motion picture camera was transferred so as to command a view of the lower side of the barrier. Then the boat was carefully towed and slid forward a little at a time until she finally gained headway, nearly jerking the rope from our hands and shot into the pool below.

The Kolb brothers emerged from Lodore Canyon on October 2, with Galloway not far behind. Putting in at Green River, Wyoming, in September, a few days after the Kolb brothers had started, Galloway was using an experimental canvas boat which he had tested earlier in Desolation and Gray canyons. He ran Hell's Half Mile without incident, facing downstream, dodging the rocks and ultimately emerging at Green River, Utah, on October 27, 1911. The journeys of the Kolb brothers and Galloway in 1911 mark the end of the pioneer river running on the Green. Nearly ninety years after William Ashley, Than Galloway demonstrated that Hell's Half Mile did not have to be portaged and lined.

In the early years of the twentieth century increasing numbers of river runners came down the Green to the big pile of boulders at the top of Hell's Half Mile. Some started out in boats but ended up walking back across the high desert to the town of Green River, Wyoming—in one notable case, stark naked! The dam surveyors came and, in 1922, the map makers of the United States Geological Survey. Four years later several graduates of Princeton University hired one of the U.S.G.S. boatmen, Elwyn Blake, to lead them on a vacation trip down the Green. Blake negotiated the initial drop in Hell's Half Mile in the first boat but became stuck in the rocks below and signaled for Lem Page, a passenger with no river running experience, to bring the second boat through. Page assumed he was "of course, crazy" to try the run, but he walked back to the boat with his heart "'damn' near in my mouth" and pushed out into the river. His account of what followed is a typical depiction of a novice's encounter with a Big Drop: ". . . here I was rushing into Hell's Half Mile [and] two big rocks just at the edge of the falls. Blake had said that it was absolutely imperative to go to the right of one of them. I had studied the falls from below and things looked entirely different from above, and I could not figure which was the rock."

Page's next statement would be repeated by many facing big rapids over the next half century: "I believe I would have given everything I possessed to have been able to turn back, but there was no turning back then." By this time Page was heading straight for the biggest rock, and he knew he must go outside of it if he could. "I never pulled so hard for the life of the boat and perhaps my own depended on it." It was a partial success. He hit the rock but rebounded to its right and headed backwards into the big hole at the base of the tongue. "For a minute the boat and I were entirely submerged in the tremendous wave below," Page continued. He popped an oarlock but replaced it, scraped over several rocks, and passed Blake who was still stalled out in midstream. Finally, victory: "Full of exhultation and relief I pulled over to a sandy beach. Hell's Half Mile was passed and I had come through it safely." Blake eventually pried himself free, and the Princeton boys were happy campers that evening. They assumed the worst in Lodore was over. But the next day in a minor rapid, a boat became seriously stuck on a mid-channel rock. Page had a nasty swim, and after failing to free the stuck boat, the group ended their vacation in a single crowded boat. At least it made for lots of stories.

A new challenger reached Hell's Half Mile on October 14, 1937. Haldane "Buzz" Holmstrom had left Green River, Wyoming, and was in the process of becoming the first man to run alone from Wyoming to the newly completed Hoover Dam. He faced hundreds of big rapids on his epic journey but lined only five. Hell's Half Mile was not one of them. In the account of his run, Holmstrom refers to himself and his boat as "we." Boatmen understand this personification; boats are true partners on the river. Charles Lindbergh also used "we" in connection with his aircraft on the 1927 flight to Paris. Holmstrom wrote:

When you understand that the speed of the current here is better than twenty-five miles an hour—it seems much faster, but that's how the Government experts measured it—and that the full force of the river rolls down at that speed, you can imagine how fast the rocks seem to be leaping toward you and how exact must be your control on the oars to dodge in and out.

Halfway down the boiling chute, we struck a submerged boulder. You can't see such things in advance in such water. Had we been going head-on, the boat would have been done for, right there, but at retarded speed the reinforced stern held. We hung for a split second, head-on in the current, then swung into the full grip of the heaped-up channel, out of control and speeding down upon the big rocks that must be avoided.

I gave the oars all I had, whirled the boat and pulled for my life. The instant we were in the clear we struck again, and this time the river seized my left oar and tore it from its socket. We hurtled sideways toward a huge boulder, and it was there that the boat itself did the trick. It slid upon the rock instead of crashing—I was thankful then for the rake I'd given her bow—spun, and slid off. By now I had the oar in place, and we eased between the remaining rocks to a safe landing below. It seemed like the boat almost chuckled out loud at me there, when we were in the clear. "Happy to oblige. But next time don't depend so much on me."

The principal problems with Hell's Half Mile are its length and its boulders. In most rapids a boatman can mark a rock or a tree on shore to designate the spot where the proper maneuver will deliver him safely down the rapid, but this is difficult in Hell's Half Mile. It is so long that one despairs of trying to keep an accurate memory of where to go and what to do. One of the great oarsmen of the 1950s and 1960s, Fred B. Eiseman, Jr., compares studying Hell's Half Mile to memorizing the complete score and all of the singing roles of *Parsifal.*

As the torrent crashed down, over, and around the boulders, boatmen memorize the first slots and the currents swirling through the rocks. They talk little and think much, their eyes moving over and over the sequence of rocks and currents and eddies. Occasionally they look too long at the whitewater and lose their nerve; others look too fleetingly and will lose their way.

Hell's Half Mile drops thirty feet in less than half a mile. The rapid is dominated by great blocks of red quartzite that have fallen from the cliff into the river to create the confusion and chaos at the top of the rapid known as Boulder Falls. That is where the trouble starts because the blocks from the canyon walls have almost dammed the river. From up on the portage trail the boulders look small; but once the boatmen have made their way to shore and leaped on some of them to study the current, they understand that looks from a distance can be deceiving. In point of fact, the boulders are enormous and constrict the only runnable channel to less than thirty feet of white fury that leads directly toward a huge midstream boulder. There is really no way to avoid coming to terms with this rock. Attempts to run left or right of it fall into the category of partial successes. Either way, you ride up on the upstream buffer wave piled up by the rock, hesitate, and if you are fortunate, slide off and on down the rapid. The entry position is crucial. The idea is to come through the accelerating water at the top of the rapid with your boat set at such an angle that its rear half remains in the fast flow moving to either side of the rock. Then, even if your bow stalls out, the stern will swing down with the current and pull you off and around. To go straight down the channel, or sideways, is your passport to a trip up and *over* the boulder. Inflatables can survive the consequent crash-landing in the reversal below, but often minus oars, gear, and passengers.

Past the rock, somehow, you look up, take a quick inventory of your belongings and companions, and glance downstream. It is then that you understand why "half mile" is in the name of this rapid. The river has widened and, necessarily, become shallower, but it continues to drop fast through a litter of rocks. In lower flows they are exposed or barely below the surface. Although breaking or popping an oar is a constant risk (and the prelude to an almost-certain wrap), there is a chance for an occasional shallow "chicken stroke." The idea is to work left away from one island but not so far as to crash into the head of the second one further downstream. At this point the rapid seems endless, but you shake and bake, pinball if necessary, and eventually reach calm water and the little beach on the left.

All this passes through your mind as you sit in the July sunshine of the high desert and scout the Green River on its way through the Canyon of Lodore. You read the water and make your calculations of its force and direction, going over in your mind how you will be positioned at this point and the one further on. Some boatmen are paid to understand these things; others do it for fun. But there is parity above a Big Drop; no one gets a free ride. So the boatmen troop back through the riparian vegetation to the boats resting quietly, for the moment, among the box elders. No one talks very much before a Big Drop. Decisions have been made, and you learn to live quietly with the fear in your stomach. Courage, after all, is not the absence of fear but its mastery. It is not, nowadays, a fear of dying so much as of failing. Rivers permit just one shot at their rapids. There are no ski lifts to take you back for another try. Blow it and you wait for the next trip to make amends. Given the numbers desiring to run western rivers, and the quota system, that could be years for a noncommercial boatman. This, then, is the moment of truth.

Knowing it, the boatmen take their time. Tie-downs are checked
again; life jackets snapped carefully. And slowly the lead boat
inches away from the bank and catches the current.

For the last boatman, captain of the "safety" boat, there is
added psychological difficulty. He must watch the others press
on ahead of him, and the wait is trying. At times he can benefit
by watching the runs of those ahead, otherwise he simply sits
above the roar of the rapid, waiting his turn while others are ex-
orcising their fears below. He may be misled by those who have
preceded him and make the same mistakes if he is not skillful in
reading the water. Moreover, he bears a special responsibility.
The last oarsman carries the safety lines to pull his comrades off
the rocks if necessary, and he sweeps the river clean to see that
all the pieces and people are appropriately rescued and carried
down. But this responsibility does not weigh as heavily as the
knowledge that when the others have run, whether there is difficulty or not, he must then take his turn and strain to run the
rapid far behind those who have gone before, only to land exhausted at the bottom just as the others have bailed their boats
and are ready to continue. In 1969 on a trip through the Canyon
of Lodore to commemorate the centennial of Powell's epic run,
Gaylord Stavely, running the first boat, succinctly summed up
the plight of the rear boatman: "The last oarsman is subject to
the most mistranslation of course and maneuvering, if there is
any, by each succeeding oarsman of the column. He's the trou-
bleshooter, charged with seeing that all other boats are finding
safe passage down the river ahead of him."

When the last oarsman pulls out there is no one left to tell
him to "have a good one." Just the rumble of the rapid and the
spray occasionally exploding above its lip. He takes four or five
strokes and pauses, studying the rocks that from river level do
not reveal the passage that seemed so obvious from the scouting
vantage point. The boat moves forward ever so slowly, creeping,
and suddenly the river catches the raft. He pulls hard to the
right to see the ledge, squares off, hits it, lines up for the midstream boulder and slides up and around with a boat half full of
water. Then the rapid begins again, and there is a constant

darting, dashing, zigzagging, and pivoting down the river
through Hell's Half Mile.

At the end of the rapid on the same beach where John Wesley Powell and Frederick Dellenbaugh camped on the second
expedition, the last boatman pulls in for congratulations or consolations. Reunited, the boatmen look back at the water tumbling over the boulders and through the rock garden. The boats
are unloaded, the cooking fire lit. Later, there is the smell of coffee. A brisk wind usually comes up the canyon, lifting away a new
song inspired by the day:

> I was ninety miles out of Denver
> In the wild and drifting snow.
> Three days across the mountains
> Seemed a lifetime to go.
>
> Green River was a-callin'
> Brown's Park layin' low.
> The ghosts of Butch and the Sundance Kid
> Are the only friends I know.
>
> Hell's Half Mile . . .
> Hell's Half Mile . . .
> I'll see you in a while.

Warm Springs

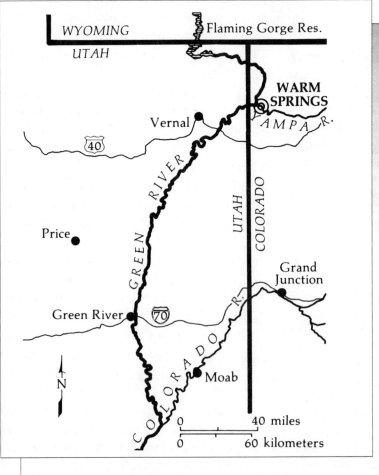

WYOMING — Flaming Gorge Res.

UTAH

WARM SPRINGS

Vernal

40

YAMPA R.

GREEN RIVER

UTAH

COLORADO

Price

Grand Junction

Green River

70

COLORADO R.

Moab

N

0		40 miles
0		60 kilometers

Chapter 4

It was 20 degrees down with the most gigantic waves and foam and holes on all sides of me. Very narrow—like trying to run down a coiled rattler's back, the rattler striking at me from all sides. I was shoved to the left bank about an inch from the cliff where a foot-wide eddy existed. For perhaps a mile I skidded and swirled and turned down this narrow line. I kept telling myself, "You can roll in this," but all the time I knew I couldn't. I expected to get jammed into the cliff but never touched it. Eventually I squirted out into a pool right side up and safe only to flip in another whirlpool before reaching shore.

WALT BLACKADAR

Before the night of June 10, 1965, there was only a minor riffle where Warm Springs Draw meets the canyon of the Yampa River in the extreme northwest corner of Colorado only a few linear miles from Hell's Half Mile on the Green. The low water of midsummer did expose two rocks, but even a child could, and sometimes did, float a boat through the wide slot between them. The few waves below the rocks were purely roller-coaster fun.

Then the big rain began. In May and June 1965 heavy rains fell on the Warm Springs watershed seventeen out of twenty-one days. The ground on the steep slopes that rise several thousand feet above the draw became supersaturated and in spots turned to the consistency of jelly. On June 10 the earth started to move. Lubricated by the heavy runoff in Warm Springs Draw, a slurry of soil, stones, uprooted trees, and drowned animals responded to the pull of gravity. As it passed the springs that gave the place its name, the thick brown soup still moved slowly and sporadically. Thereafter it picked up both speed and size, building into a wall of semisolid debris about fifteen feet high.

Warm Springs Draw widens into a

sizeable delta just before its confluence with the Yampa, but such was the momentum of the flash flood that it hardly paused. Crashing into the Yampa, the mass of rock and gravel filled the river bed and rolled up against the cliff on the opposite bank.

For a few hours the Yampa was completely dammed. Campers downstream at Echo Park watched with astonishment, especially in view of the heavy rains, as the level of the river dropped quickly to a trickle. The condition was temporary, however; pooling up behind the debris dam at Warm Springs, the Yampa's force became irresistible. Sometime in the early morning hours of June 11, 1965, the river breached the natural dam and, with a guttural roar, resumed its accustomed task of carrying the continent toward the Pacific. After several hours of rapid erosion there was a ragged S-shaped channel dropping steeply through the remains of the landslide. Enormous waves and holes studded its half-mile length. A Big Drop had been born.

Daylight on June 11 found several river parties moving down the Yampa toward Warm Springs, completely unaware of the changes ahead. The first boats belonged to Hatch River Expeditions, one of the oldest companies in the river-outfitting business. Hatch's twenty-seven-foot pontoons, powered by oars, were usually more than adequate to negotiate the relatively mild whitewater in the meandering sandstone canyons of the Yampa. The Hatch party, consisting of a troop of boy scouts from Denver, two adult leaders, and two experienced boatmen, had put in at Deerlodge Park, about fifty river miles above Warm Springs. For several days they marveled at the Yampa's sculpture. At one point the river doubled back on itself so sharply that a float of seven miles was required to reach a point less than a linear mile away—a bowknot bend. Some of the scouts scrambled over the low divide on foot and waited for the boats to come around. Another highlight was where the Yampa undercut its bordering cliffs so deeply as to produce massive overhangs. Manganese oxide left black stripes on the tawny rock. Sliding close to the base of these "tiger walls," the river runners felt as if they were in a cave. At the Grand Overhang, a stone dropped straight down from the top of the thousand-foot cliff would land on the Yampa's *opposite* bank.

The heavy rains soaked the camping gear of the Hatch party, but the boatmen were professionals who knew how to cope with such conditions. The new rapid at Warm Springs was something else.

Al Holland rowed one of the Hatch boats, Les Oldham the other. About a half mile above Warm Springs Draw, Holland and Oldham drifted together to discuss the fact that the river seemed strange to them compared with previous trips. They had no way of knowing that it had risen and slowed behind the new rapid. Rounding the last bend above the draw, their confusion turned to anxiety. A roar that, in Holland's words, "sounded like a locomotive" echoed up the canyon. Still uncertain what had happened, the boatmen continued to drift downstream along the left-hand shore, peering ahead through the spitting rain. They made no attempt to row to the right, land, and scout ahead. It may have been that the initial drop of the new rapid was so sharp that the boatmen's river-level perspective revealed only space and distant tailwaves. Or perhaps they were unable to act against their knowledge that there just was no major rapid at Warm Springs. In any event they continued past the point at which they might have pulled their heavy rigs out of the current.

Les Oldham entered the tongue first and accelerated down it directly toward an enormous hole. Recognizing the danger, he pulled frantically on his left oar in an effort to direct the pontoon right of the hole. He succeeded, but the force of his pull broke the pin holding the oar to the frame, and Oldham's own power catapulted him backward into the river. Miraculously, the boat wallowed through right side up.

In the second pontoon Al Holland watched Oldham being snapped from his boat, then turned his attention to waves he remembered as over twenty feet high. It must have been a riverman's nightmare: floating on what was supposed to be quiet water, he was suddenly fighting the Yampa for his life. Holland won; Oldham did not.

After successfully running Warm Springs, Holland pulled to shore, organized the passengers on both boats, and began to search for Oldham. After several hours it became apparent that their search was for a corpse. Moving on in rain and silence to Echo Park, the party reported the fatality. Someone recalled that at the time he entered the rapid, Oldham was sitting on his life preserver. Seventeen days later Oldham's body washed ashore at Island Park.

Following the report of the drowning, National Park Service rangers dispatched a plane to warn other boats on the Yampa above Warm Springs. Flying low over the startled river parties, the pilot dropped a sealed container into the river. The note inside told of the new Big Drop and the way it had claimed its first life. Shaken, Dee Holladay and other boatmen approached Warm Springs with extreme caution. Hugging the right bank, they landed on the upper edge of the debris fan extending from the draw and walked down through the jumble of logs and rocks to read the whitewater ahead.

Warm Springs is one of the longest and technically most difficult rapids in the Colorado drainage. Its most frightening aspect is its ability to flip in at least eight different holes. This is in marked contrast to many Big Drops (Rainie Falls and Big Mallard are examples), where the major problem is concentrated in a few dozen feet. At the top of Warm Springs a short, fast tongue ends in very large but still regularly shaped waves. Holland described them as "twenty-footers," but objectively seen they are only about half that height. The entrance waves lead directly into a maelstrom of whitewater on the left at the foot of Warm Springs Cliff. The holes here are formidable, virtual waterfalls behind the nearly exposed boulders. Rocks washed into the Yampa by the 1965 landslide are one cause of the chaos. Another is the slabs and cornices fallen from Warm Springs Cliff.

There is no ambiguity about how the upper part of Warm Springs must be run. Since no boat can count on surviving the left side, it is imperative to pull off the tongue to the right and skirt the edge of the cliffside holes. The maneuver sounds easier than it is. The Yampa thrusts boats left, toward the cliff, and to overcome this force it is necessary to row powerfully in large waves. This means the boat must be angled to the right. As a result, it strikes the waves at a dangerous oblique angle. Hundreds of pounds of water slosh in, making control more difficult. Moreover, the big waves prevent oars or sweeps from obtaining a good grip on the water. At the top of a wave a boat sits on a pinnacle, and oars cannot reach the water. In the troughs the walls of water are so close together that it is almost impossible to stroke and recover an oar. Only the most careful timing permits a boatman to row at all. To panic and flail wildly is to remain in the grip of the main flow and headed directly for trouble.

If Warm Springs Rapid ended with the initial big waves and the holes along the cliff, it would be imposing enough. In fact, two-thirds of the rapid and several major obstacles are still to come. The first of these are several midstream rocks that force boatmen to pull far right, almost against the right bank. This puts them in the line of a long, sharp boulder bar extending into the river from the same right bank. Particularly with boats heavy from water shipped in the upper part of the rapid, the rocky bar is hard to avoid. Ungainly pontoons repeatedly strike it sideways, and some roll over with astonishing ease almost within touching distance of spectators on shore. A smaller rowed boat can miss this bar, but only if the boatman accurately calculates his position in the rapid, anticipates far enough upstream, and leans into his pull left with every ounce of strength.

The price of missing the right-side boulder bar is to enter once again the main current left of the center of the river. Ahead are two enormous rock barriers, just awash in high water. Below them are still other huge, barely submerged rocks, most of which have tumbled from Warm Springs Cliff in the last decade. The left side of the river is again disaster. So once more the boatmen force tired muscles to spin their rigs and pull out of the main flow to the right. The boats that reach this point in the rapid with broken or lost oars or minus a boatman (who may have been tossed from his seat like Les Oldham) or too heavy with water to maneuver will almost certainly upset behind or, in low water, wrap around these rocks. What all this means is that a perfect run of Warm Springs is a right-left-right slalom. Each move must be made against the main force of the river and in waves of formidable size. It's big water and technical water at once.

Just as he had been the first white man to look with a scientist's eye at Hell's Half Mile, Satan's Gut, and Lava Falls, John Wesley Powell also led the way into the lower canyon of the Yampa. Of course, Warm Springs Rapid did not then exist as a Big Drop, but Powell formed an accurate conception of the geography and geology of the region. On June 20, 1869, Powell and his men rowed up the Yampa from its confluence with the Green River in Echo Park. Taking full advantage of eddies and backwaters, their boats rounded several mile-long bends. Near Warm Springs Draw they abandoned the effort and landed on a sandbar below a break in the golden cliffs which Powell used to gain access to the rim of the Yampa's canyon.

According to his journal for June 20, Powell walked "over long stretches of naked sandstone, crossing gulches now and then." It was a crisp, sparkling day in the mountains. "The air is singularly clear today," Powell reported. "Mountains and buttes stand in sharp outline, valleys stretch out in perspective, and I can look down into the deep canyon gorges and see gleaming waters."

Looking northeast from this vantage, Powell could see the snow-capped Wind River range as it defined the Continental Divide in central Wyoming. Only a hundred linear miles distant, the Wind Rivers were actually beyond the starting point of Powell's river journey three weeks earlier. Farther away and more to the east, he noted the highlands in the vicinity of Rabbit Ears Pass, Colorado. The Yampa rises in the high meadows and pine forests of this section of the Divide. But the view west was the most imposing. Beyond the sagebrush-dotted benchlands and yellow cliffs of the Yampa's inner gorge, Powell faced the Uinta Range. Trending east-west across Utah and into western Colorado, the Uinta uplift runs squarely across the courses of the Green and Yampa rivers.

The few whites who had seen this landscape before Powell could not understand why the rivers had cut canyons through the Uintas rather than veering around them. The explorer-priests of Spain, Escalante and Dominguez, remarked in 1776 on the way the combined Yampa and Green came directly out of a "split" mountain. A half century later, in 1825, William Ashley and his company of trappers, scouring the Yampa and the Green for fur, understood no better the seemingly illogical geography of rivers that ran directly into, rather than around, mountain ranges.

Powell came next, and standing above Warm Springs Draw on that clear day in June 1869, he found the explanation: the rivers came first. The mountains rose later, after the Yampa and the Green had already established their courses off the Continental Divide. As the great Uinta uplift occurred, the rivers cut deeper and deeper through the rising skin of the earth. What Powell saw below him were the entrenched meanders of a formerly lazy valley river. The ancestral Yampa's loops were now incised in Weber sandstone a thousand feet deep. Powell scrambled back down to his boats with the essential thesis later scientists would use to interpret the region's geology.

After Powell's short venture up the Yampa in 1869, the river was not run again until 1909, when Nathaniel Galloway and his young son Parley floated the entire Yampa Canyon. Characteristically river wise, Galloway chose the high water of June to make the trip. He wanted to run the Yampa before the decreasing flow of summer transformed it into an unfloatable rock garden. Moreover, Galloway had a date with Julius Stone to run the Green and Colorado from Wyoming to California in the early fall.

The shy Galloway did not care to surround his remarkable river-running feats with fanfare. This was not true of a team sponsored by the *Denver Post* in 1928 for the second descent of the Yampa. Headlines screamed about how the four-man party made one harrowing escape after another on what was erroneously labeled the first descent of the Yampa. One story detailed the "tragic" loss of a boat and equipment. There was no mention that the real tragedy was the *Post's* choice of a time to run the Yampa. In August the river was predictably low and rock-choked. The four men struggled along, often dragging their boats. The final article about their trip appeared under the headline, "Glad to Get Home Alive!" Galloway would have been amused.

Few who run Warm Springs Rapid today are aware how close the 1965 flash flood came to pouring its debris into a man-made lake rather than a living river. In the early 1950s the United States Bureau of Reclamation almost built a dam—Echo Park— on the Green River two miles below the Yampa confluence. The resulting reservoir would have inundated the canyons of both the Green and the Yampa, and the site of Warm Springs Rapid would have been several hundred feet under the water of a lake. Another Big Drop, Hell's Half Mile, would also have been lost.

At the outset it seemed that the canyons of the Yampa and the Green would be safe, protected as part of Dinosaur National Monument, which is administered by the National Park Service. The unusual name of this reserve came from the discovery in 1909 by the Carnegie Museum's Earl Douglas of a remarkable deposit of dinosaur bones on the northeastern slope of the Uinta Basin. Geologists believe that 140 million years ago the area was a sandbar in an ancient stream. The bodies of dinosaurs, some as long as eighty-four feet, came to rest on the bar and were covered by muds and sands that, over the eons, totaled five thousand feet. During this time, fossilization occurred as silica replaced the organic materials in the bones. Then, in another chapter of earth history, erosion peeled off the five thousand feet of sedimentary rock. Douglas arrived at the precise tick of geologic time that found the bones exposed on the surface of the earth just as they were 140 million years before.

Excited by what turned out to be one of the world's greatest collections of dinosaur remains, Douglas and other scientists urged their preservation. President Woodrow Wilson responded in 1915 by designating an 80-acre Dinosaur National Monument around the deposit. No rivers were involved at all. But in 1938 President Franklin D. Roosevelt enlarged the reserve to 200,000 acres. Now about one hundred miles of the Green and Yampa canyons were included as well as the surrounding benchland and peaks reaching nine thousand feet. The Colorado-Utah state line almost bisected the new monument.

In the 1940s the Bureau of Reclamation began plans for a ten-dam, billion-dollar Colorado River Storage Project. One of the key structures was slated for the lower end of Echo Park. By the early 1950s the controversy over Echo Park Dam had reached nationwide proportions, involving Americans in a debate over protected wilderness very similar to the 1913 one concerning Hetch Hetchy Valley and the Tuolumne River in Yosemite National Park. (See the earlier chapter, "Clavey Falls.") In both cases the principal issue was whether development should be permitted in an area (Dinosaur National Monument) specifically dedicated to preserve the natural environment.

On a deeper level, the Echo Park controversy brought the American people face to face with perplexing questions about the meaning of progress and of happiness. In many eyes Echo Park was a showdown between priorities. "Let's open this to its ultimate and inevitable extent," one dam opponent urged, "and let's settle . . . once and for all time . . . whether we may have . . . wilderness areas . . . in these United States." Everyone realized that as Dinosaur went so would go a number of pending applications for economic exploitation of national parks. "Perhaps the stage is set," another preservationist remarked, "for a full dress performance by all those . . . who are protecting the West's recreational and wilderness values."

One of the first salvos in the Echo Park fight came from the facile pen of Bernard DeVoto. Writing in the *Saturday Evening Post* for July 22, 1950, DeVoto opened with a question: "Shall we let them ruin our national parks?" He argued that if the integrity of Dinosaur were compromised in the interest of economic development, no unit of the national park system would ever again be safe. In weighing the value of wild canyons and their rivers, DeVoto urged his countrymen to take their uniqueness into account. Flatwater impoundments were plentiful. You could, DeVoto pointed out, sail or waterski on dozens of them in the West. Wild rivers large enough for whitewater boating were rare, and the Yampa and the Green were two of the best. DeVoto noted that people travel across the continent to run the Dinosaur rivers, then asked rhetorically, "Would you drive 2,000 miles to sail a dinghy there?" In DeVoto's eyes the whole nation was the loser in an exchange of a spectacular and rare recreational opportunity for a commonplace one. He rejected totally the Bureau of Reclamation's contention that Echo Park Dam would improve the recreational value of Dinosaur National Monument.

The bureau quickly rose in response. Its elaborate color brochure argued that the reservoir would increase the accessibility and even the beauty of the canyons. "Echo Park Dam," the developers asserted, "will create a playground for millions." The statement ignored the fact that for those who love wilderness, "play" and "millions" are contradictory. The Sierra Club and the Wilderness Society followed this line of reasoning in contending that in the interests of diversity and of fairness there should be opportunities for those who coveted solitude, danger, and wildness. It was a mistake to reduce national parks and monuments to amusement parks on the basis of some twisted definition of democracy. As in the case of great art or music, only a minority might appreciate wild rivers, but that minority surely had a right to a small fraction of the American landscape. And what about the rights of natural ecosystems to exist unimpaired regardless of their utility to humans?

Such arguments received wide distribution in the film *Wilderness River Trail*, produced by Charles Eggert and pioneer whitewater doryman Martin Litton in February 1954. Shown to thousands, including some members of Congress, it dramatized what was at stake in the canyons of the Yampa and the Green. Another broadside in the Echo Park battle was a book edited by novelist and historian Wallace Stegner, *This Is Dinosaur: Echo Park Country and Its Magic Rivers*. Like the film, this book was a potent weapon in the defense of the American wilderness. Preservationists of the 1950s were determined not to lose Dinosaur as they had lost Hetch Hetchy forty years earlier by failing to state their case effectively.

Wilderness defenders also showed that since Hetch Hetchy they had learned how to play the game of politics more skillfully. The leading conservation organizations pooled their efforts in several lobbying agencies and prepared for congressional hearings with great care. Besides making a case for wild rivers, the preservationists schooled themselves in the techniques of power politics. By the end of 1955 the entire issue boiled down to the fact that the friends of Dinosaur had the support of enough congressmen to stalemate the *entire* Colorado River Storage Project indefinitely. It then became a case of simple political horse-trading. The price of passing the project was the deletion of the dam in the national monument. Realizing they were trapped, the advocates of western water development grudgingly settled for less than the full loaf. When the Colorado River Storage Project became a reality on April 11, 1956, the act of authorization contained the stipulation that "no dam or reservoir constructed under the authorization of the Act shall be within any National Park or Monument." Plans for a dam were shifted from Echo Park further downstream to Glen Canyon which was not in the national park system.

Although Glen Canyon Dam came to be hated by river lovers, the 1956 defeat of Echo Park Dam marked the finest hour in the history of the American wilderness movement to that date. The loss of Hetch Hetchy had in some measure been avenged, the national park idea reaffirmed. Moreover, success in defending Dinosaur encouraged preservationists to press for still more positive protection of wilderness. In the same year as the Echo Park victory Congress began consideration of the National Wilderness Preservation Act. In 1964, after eight years of complex and often bitter negotiation, America constructed the world's first legally authorized system designed to protect, specifically, wilderness. The Yampa Canyon, as part of the roadless backcountry of a national monument, was ultimately included in the National Wilderness Preservation System. Whether it will actually remain wilderness, country capable of giving visitors a wilderness experience, is not as certain.

The problem, as on many other whitewater rivers in the West, is people. The wilderness qualities of the Yampa are very close to being loved to death. The Yampa is exceptionally vulnerable to overcrowding. It is relatively accessible; a day's drive brings river runners from the metropolitan areas of Salt Lake City and Denver. Except for Warm Springs Rapid, which can be portaged, the Yampa is relatively easy to run. A novice can muddle through leaving only a little paint on an occasional rock to testify to his troubles. But the biggest factor in the crowding of this undammed river is the way that the boating season is confined to the runoff months of May and June. Even with a permit system in effect, the Yampa is heavily used during the prime time. Campsites are scheduled in advance of river trips, and two or more parties often share the same site. There are outhouses and picnic tables. It is rare when the boats of other parties are not in sight most of the day.

Despite all this, a 1973 Utah State University study revealed that almost 50 percent of river runners believed the Yampa had "about the right level of use." This finding is disturbing as far as the future of the Yampa as a wilderness river is concerned. What seems to be occurring on the Yampa is a tendency sociologists call "displacement." People who like wilderness are being displaced by people who simply like to have fun outdoors. The change parallels the evolving nature of river running everywhere from a solitary, risky, expeditionary kind of activity to a form of mass recreation comparable to downhill skiing. River running continues to grow, but lovers of wild rivers who have the time and money now travel to Ethiopia, Nepal, Alaska, Chile, and Peru. There the sport is still young, the local people uninterested, and the rivers empty and wild.

As the displacement process continues, those running the Yampa are increasingly people-tolerant. They do not care if their river trip is not a wilderness trip. The Utah State University study found that 56.6 percent of the sample of Yampa boaters interviewed indicated that they made the trip for "fun and games, adventure, excitement." Only 43.4 percent defined their goal as "wilderness, solitude, back to nature." Fifteen years later with the river even more crowded, that figure is likely much lower. It is probably true today that most river runners on the Yampa are not disturbed by the presence of large numbers of people any more than they would be at a football game.

Amidst all of this new controversy over the inundation of wilderness by people rather than reservoirs, Warm Springs Rapid preserves an element of honesty. A ski resort may be crowded, with lift lines two hours long, but the expert trails with their six-foot moguls still exist. Although Warm Springs has moderated over the years as the Yampa displaces its rocks, high water (like the 37,000 cubic feet per second that thundered down the river in June 1984) brings out the muscle in the rapid. Each season Warm Springs wipes out a surprisingly high percentage of the boats that start down its tongue and gives a considerable number of river runners the unnerving experience of swimming a Big Drop. The regular action of the big waves below the tongue seems to mesmerize oarsmen, and they forget about the holes waiting downstream. Frozen to the oars, they ride on to certain upsets. On many trips Warm Springs claims half the boats in a party. A few years ago seven rafts entered the rapid in a neat formation and seven rafts floated out at the bottom upside down—still in formation. There was a lot of adventure swimming that day. Even the professionals continue to have trouble in Warm Springs. The big pontoons some of them use lack the quickness in changing direction that success in this drop demands. Recently an experienced commercial boatman, a Green Beret veteran from Vietnam, rolled his rig at the top of the rapid. In the next three hundred yards Warm Springs picked his boat clean: oars, frame, packs, and people ended up scattered along several miles of shoreline.

Regulations and crowds are part of the Yampa today, but so is Warm Springs. When all is said and done, it still provides the opportunity to be challenged, and perhaps overwhelmed, by nature. For many this remains the essential part of the wilderness experience.

Satan's Gut

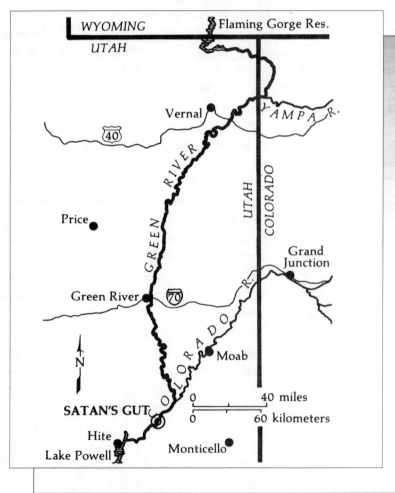

WYOMING

Flaming Gorge Res.

UTAH

Vernal

YAMPA R.

40

GREEN RIVER

UTAH

COLORADO

Price

Grand
Junction

Green River

70

COLORADO R.

COLORADO

Moab

N

SATAN'S GUT

0   40 miles
0   60 kilometers

Hite

Lake Powell

Monticello

Chapter 5

This is a day when life and the world seem to be standing still—only time and the river flowing past the mesas.

EDITH WHARTON

Historically, men have marveled at Grand Canyon but feared Cataract. In the labyrinth of canyons lacing the Colorado Plateau, Cataract Canyon is the most deceptive and devious. Above are the placid waters of the Green and Colorado rivers, whose serenity lures boatmen into unwarranted confidence and belies the turbulence ahead. Below Cataract the blue waters of Lake Powell shimmer in the sun, having drowned the spectacular rapid at Dark Canyon and the scenic wonders of Narrow and Glen canyons. But in Cataract Canyon the Colorado River descends eighty feet in less than four miles. It is the biggest cumulative drop along any stretch of the Colorado.

Cataract is also the deepest canyon in Utah, its walls towering two thousand feet above the river. They are steep walls, precipitous, moving upward in ledges which mirror the step-like descent of the river below. There are few tributaries in Cataract Canyon, but during the thunderstorms on the dry plateau above, the runoff, reddened by the desert soil, will plunge over the cliffs in dramatic vermillion waterfalls. They swell the river as it moves inexorably between the canyon walls to three contiguous rapids known collectively as the Big Drop. The third and biggest is Satan's Gut.

The first part of the Big Drop consists of big rolling waves down a curving staircase of violent water. Particularly at highwater flows of May and June, the emphasis in on *big*! Get slightly sideways and they can flip you like the proverbial pancake. And for your next act there is the opportunity for a very spectacular swim of more than a mile. Run the first part properly, however, and it is not difficult to pull out on the left above the Big Drop's second stage. Walking down the shoreline at medium to high flows, your attention is riveted on one of the biggest holes in western rivers. Dee Holladay calls it "Niagara." A house-sized rock has rolled from the cliffs and lodged in the right center of the main flow. The obvious course is left but with a quick cutback to the right to avoid a long ledge-hole. What follows are some truly enormous waves, and the higher the water, the bigger they get. The wave chain leads into a widening and slowing of the Colorado above the third part of the rapid: Satan's Gut. Most boatmen scout it while they look at the second part because sometimes there is no alternative but to run them without pause. The Gut is, at first sight, staggering. Knees weaken and mouths go dry. Although the upper canyon may have been no problem for today's boats and boatmen, you suddenly know the reason for Cataract's formidable reputation. The legend still has substance.

On the left huge, angular blocks of limestone litter the shore, and they continue under water. Satan's Gut is the result. The Colorado drops and surges over and through a picket line of rocks. At higher flows boatmen favor a right-side entry and take their chances on the big exploding waves in the middle of the rapid. Lower water demands more finesse in route selection. It finally comes down to hitting a silken thread of water on the left side that creates a watery ridge between two of the nastiest holes in the West. It is obvious immediately that safe passage is along that yard-wide thread. Enter a few feet left or right and you will be severely thrashed, probably flipped, and perhaps recycled for a dangerously long time. Boatmen try to block such thoughts from their minds. Inner rowing: be optimistic, keep a positive mental attitude, think success. They search for the "cue" or "key" that will guide them to the proper entry point. What they find is a little dimple on brown enamel water. As the river accelerates it kicks up an insignificant wave, no more than four inches in height, but one with great meaning to those who would run Satan's Gut. Put it under the middle of your boat and you pass between those devilish, churning cauldrons.

Easier said, of course, than done. The Colorado is really moving by the time you reach the marker wave; the objective is to spot it far enough away so as to make the necessary corrections in time. So the boatmen rise to their feet, poised, only their eyes darting. Then, with the die cast, it's time to sit down, straighten out, and go for the gusto. Correctly done, it's over in a flash. You hardly notice the boiling holes, and relieved tensions explode into screams as you buck through the tailwaves toward, regrettably, the flat water of Lake Powell. It's the boffo performance in Cataract Canyon.

The rapid has been there for eons but not its vivid name. In fact, in the early days river runners simply referred to the rapids in Cataract in numerical sequence—first, fifth, and so forth. The Big Drop began with Rapid 21. There were forty-six big rapids in all before Glen Canyon Dam. In August 1952 Kenny Ross, one of the best of the first generation of commercial boatmen, was leading a trip down Cataract Canyon. After running the ridge down the left side third stage of the Big Drop, one of Ross's passengers exclaimed that it was like passing through "Satan's Gut." Ross perpetuated the name, and it caught on in river circles, but with some ambiguity. It has been applied to the whole third part. Kenny Ross's intent, however, was to associate the devil's intestines with that thin, smooth tube of water between the horrible holes of the left side. Ironically, for boatmen, Satan's Gut is also a highway to the heaven of calm water.

Cataract Canyon is known as "the graveyard of the Colorado" because so many early river runners died in its rapids. They left pathetic memorials to their troubles scratched onto the rocks alongside whitewater. The place was hard even on survivors. Those who lived after losing their boats faced the grim prospect of climbing up Cataract's decomposing limestone walls. There were no trails. And once on top the men were in the middle of nowhere. Cataract Canyon was and still is surrounded by some of the wildest, least populated country in the contiguous forty-eight states. Some died on the rim for want of the very substance that caused their initial problems: water.

There is little evidence of Indian familiarity with Cataract. In contrast to the Grand Canyon, where the ruins of the Anasazi are common, Cataract seems to have been avoided. The first white mountain men in the region sought beaver pelts and gold, but all but a few followed the Indian example. One exception was the enigmatic Denis Julien who left his name, the date 1836, and what appears to be the shape of a boat carved on riverside rocks both above and below the whitewater reach. No one will ever know for sure if this far-ranging trapper with the French antecedents actually tried to run the river. But thirty-three years later John Wesley Powell led eight men to the great confluence where the Green River, flowing south from Wyoming's Wind River Mountains, met a river then called the "Grand" to form the Colorado.

Sensing that he was at a major landmark of the Southwest, and suspecting rough going ahead, Powell and his group camped at the confluence for several days in July 1869. They caulked the boats, dried their food, which had been seriously diminished up at Disaster Falls in the Canyon of Lodore, and gazed at the bizarre formations on the canyon rim called by the Indians *Toom'-pin wu-near' Tu-weap*, the Land of Standing Rocks. This was "a whole land of naked rocks," Powell reported, "with giant forms carved on it: cathedral-shaped buttes, towering hundreds or thousands of feet; cliffs that cannot be scaled, and canyon walls that shrink the river into insignificance, with vast, hollow domes, and tall pinnacles, and shafts set on the verge overhead, and all highly colored—buff, gray, red, brown, and chocolate; never lichened; never moss-covered; but bare and often polished."

On July 19 Powell and George Y. Bradley climbed out on the east side of the canyon across the river from camp. To the west rose the Land of Standing Rocks, and beyond stood mighty "cliffs where the soaring eagle is lost to view ere he reached the summit." To the northeast were the towering peaks of the La Sal Mountains, green with pine and aspen and capped by snow. In all directions there is "but a wilderness of rocks; deep gorges, where the rivers are lost below cliffs and towers and pinnacles; and ten thousand strangely carved forms in every direction; and beyond them mountains blending with the clouds."

Two years later Powell came back to the confluence on his second expedition down the Grand Canyon and lingered another five days in the same camp. Frederick S. Dellenbaugh thought it a dreary place, "with no footing but a few sand-banks that are being constantly cut away and reformed by the whirling current." Today tamarisk, an exotic newcomer to the riparian vegetation, forms an impenetrable wall beyond the sand of the beach where Powell and his men camped amidst scrawny hackberry trees and weeds. Few people camp there today, but those who enjoy history will sometimes stop to watch the meeting of the waters and think about the whitewater pioneers.

On the first expedition in 1869, not knowing the dangers that lay beyond, Powell felt there was something ominous and elemental about the meeting of the two greatest rivers of the American Southwest. The rocks told him. Even to a novice the confluence of two large rivers signifies heavier water, and to gaze downstream into constricting and rising walls, one instinctively knows that the days of quiet water are now behind. Powell and his men left the confluence on July 21, 1869, and were in trouble from the start. Powell noted that "the river is rough, and bad rapids, in close succession, are found." After Powell's boat, the *Emma Dean*, was swamped in one of Cataract's first rapids and its oars lost, they became more cautious. Resin was collected to caulk the boats whose seams had been opened by the power of the water crashing over rocks and rising into standing waves. The oars were replaced by shaping cottonwood logs taken from piles of driftwood. On July 24 Powell reached the top of Mile Long Rapid, where huge boulders choked the channel and the twenty-foot-per-mile descent starts. Painfully they portaged the supplies across the boulder-strewn shore and then lined the boats down along the shore.

The following day Powell's party came to the twenty-first rapid. They attempted to run it and at the outset the *Emma Dean* was caught in a whirlpool and again lost her oars. Putting ashore, all the boats were lined safely down through Satan's Gut. Powell was more fortunate than those who followed.

In 1875 Powell produced his report, "Explorations of the Colorado River of the West and Its Tributaries." It purported to be an account of the 1869 trip, but was in fact a composite of the journals of his first expedition and his second expedition of 1871-1872, intermixed with his magazine articles in *Scribners Monthly*. Scholars have criticized Powell for taking liberties with history, but his purpose was to attract the attention of the public and particularly the Congress of the United States to convince them to grant additional funds for geological research. He was astoundingly successful: his report created a sensation in the Congress, which ultimately rewarded him with the directorship of the United States Geological Survey. The public was also delighted that a government report could be filled with such adventure and excitement.

John Wesley Powell's reputation in the 1870s was comparable to that of the astronauts a century later. He had also journeyed into the unknown. One of the fascinated readers of his report was Robert Brewster Stanton, a college student at Miami University in Ohio. Stanton looked up from Powell's pages and dreamed of the beauties of the Colorado River and its great canyons with vertical walls set a mile deep in the earth. He talked with his fellow students about grandiose schemes of building bridges across the chasm, and these ideas led him to a career in civil engineering. His subsequent work, which included a reconnaissance for the Southwest and Atlantic and Pacific railroads, brought him recognition for his talents as an engineer.

This was the great age of railroad building in the West, and Americans left their covered wagons to press westward on iron rails. The golden spike was driven at Promontory Point, Utah, on May 10, 1869, to link the Pacific ocean with the Atlantic. Just two weeks later John Wesley Powell set out from the town of Green River, Wyoming, to explore the canyons of the Colorado. He used the new railroad to transport his boats and supplies to the put-in on the Green.

In the 1880s a prospector, S.S. Harper, made his way across southern Colorado and central and northern Arizona to follow the line of the Atlantic and Pacific railway survey which Robert Stanton had previously carried out. Under the bright moon and stars of those crystalline nights on the great redrock plateau country, Harper conceived of a railroad to the west coast that followed the waters of the Colorado River, a route more level and, he imagined, practical than the mountain ranges he had so painfully overcome. He made his way back to Denver to sell his scheme. These were bonanza years in which men made and lost vast sums of money. Speculators from all over the world were investing in the magic rails that took the course of empire westward beyond the hundredth meridian to the Pacific ocean. The West was a land of adventurers, hardy outdoorsmen, scouts, and surveyors plumbing their way to the Pacific shore. It was a land of businessmen and investors, too—smart men in swank suits who congregated in Denver to put together the schemes that they hoped would make them rich. Stanton's star was about to rise.

One of the entrepreneurs was Frank M. Brown, a Maine man by birth who grew up in Washington, D.C., and worked in Alaska for the Hudson's Bay Company. He had heard of the great mineral boom in Leadville, Colorado, and arrived there to be put in charge of the Farwell group of mines at Independence. He established a reputation for integrity, and his charisma attracted a wide friendship that the Denver *Republican* described as more precious than gold. He was known as "a man of force, with daring and enterprise." The Brown Palace Hotel, which still graces downtown Denver, was one monument to his success. He hoped another would be a Colorado River railroad. After all, he thought, the waters of thousands of years had done the work of grading the perfect railroad bed. Frank Brown set out to turn the vague scheme of S.S. Harper into reality.

On March 25, 1889, Frank Brown formed the Denver, Colorado Canyon, and Pacific Railroad Company. Three days later the survey team, under the direction of Frank C. Kendrick, began the journey from Grand Junction down the Colorado past the Mormon community of Moab and, on easy water, to the Green River. Reaching the confluence Kendrick's party made their way up the Green to the railroad town then called Blake, but now known as Green River, Utah. Here they were met by Brown and his team of sixteen men who were prepared to go all the way to the Pacific. Brown had advertised for a chief engineer to conduct the survey to the coast, and in the middle of April hired Robert Brewster Stanton.

Frank Brown never appreciated the power of moving water. He had talked with John Wesley Powell, who described with his customary eloquence the danger of river running down the Colorado, but Brown was not impressed. His boats were small, narrow, and lightweight compared to those of Powell. They looked superb, sleek, and fast and would have been ideal for rowing on lakes, but they were not up to the pounding of Cataract Canyon. Like most beginners on the river, Brown's men brought too much personal equipment packed in cumbersome zinc-lined boxes, and not enough food and supplies. When loaded, the six boats were so heavy that Brown had to lash a barge together in order to carry all the unnecessary gear. This awkward raft was difficult to control even on flat water and totally unmanageable in rapids.

The expedition left Green River, Utah, on May 25, 1889, and in four days floated down to the confluence with the Colorado. This was going to be easy, Brown thought. On May 30 they drifted two miles along the left bank below the confluence to the brink of Cataract Canyon. Stanton, the realist, later wrote, "It would be a great relief, if it were possible, for me to blot out all remembrance of the two weeks following this evening of May 31st." Stanton's forebodings were deepened by his engineer's calculation of the impact between Brown's light cedar boats and the hard rocks of Cataract Canyon. But the construction of the boats was not Brown's greatest mistake: he had brought no life preservers, and later in the Grand Canyon this omission would prove fatal.

Like many who have followed, Brown and his men were in trouble from the beginning of Cataract Canyon. At the top of the first rapid, known today as Brown Betty after Brown's kitchen boat, the cumbersome raft loaded with provisions was swept away and careened down the river to be destroyed on the rocks below. This disaster was followed by others. Brown's boat capsized, and he and two other men were swept down for more than a mile and a half before they were able to make their way to shore. Thereafter, they worked their way down through the canyon, portaging most of the rapids, sometimes losing the boats only to catch them below in the eddies, filled to the gunwales with water.

On June 7 the *Brown Betty* was again upset, this time losing the remaining cooking gear. One boat was so badly battered that it was good only to be broken up to provide wood to repair the others. From one day to the next the expedition struggled down the canyon, portaging the supplies and lining the boats around the rocks along the shore. The boats were almost uncontrollable; time and again lines slipped and tore skin from the hands of the crew. On June 11 their last ration of beans disappeared into the river and on June 12 the coffee pot sank. The next day they faced the Big Drop at its most dangerous time, mid-June. The full flood of the Colorado was hitting the biggest drop on the river, Satan's Gut.

It took Brown and his men two days to line the boats and portage the supplies down through the Big Drop, and by June 15 all that was left were four boats and little food. Stanton took charge. He had the remaining supplies prepared and divided into sixteen portions, enough to last a week. The party continued down the remaining rapids of Cataract Canyon to the quiet waters of Narrow Canyon where they were resupplied by provisions brought up from Dandy Crossing, where the prospector Cass Hite had settled in 1883 to mine for gold. Regrouped and newly supplied with food, Brown's expedition continued on mild water through Glen Canyon to Lee's Ferry. By July 9 Brown had gone overland to Kanab and returned with three more boats

and supplies sufficient to allow him to continue on his quest for
a water-level railroad route to the Pacific.

Below Lee's Ferry was Marble Canyon, where they portaged
Badger and Soap Creek rapids, camping at the foot of Soap
Creek. The following day Brown's boat capsized a half mile below Soap. Having no life preserver, Brown was drowned in
whirlpools, leaving only his notebook floating on the river.
Stunned, the party spent the remaining daylight vainly seeking
the body, which never was found. Three days later a second boat
capsized, and two other members of the expedition, Peter Hans-
borough and the black steward, Henry Richards, were drowned.
The deaths completely destroyed the sagging morale of the
Brown expedition, and Stanton cached his gear in a cave and left
the river at the first available point, South Canyon. To his credit,
he did return in 1890 with stouter boats to complete the railroad
survey that no one ever used.

After the railway builders, the miners came to Cataract
Canyon. In 1891 James S. Best led a party of nine men in two
boats. They were prospectors setting out to make their way down
the Colorado seeking minerals and wealth. They drifted past the
confluence and then, like Brown and Stanton, found trouble. At
the top of Mile Long Rapid opposite Range Canyon, one of their
boats smashed into a large rock in mid-river and broke into
pieces. Though the men were able to save themselves, they lost
valuable supplies and the boat. Nine men were now left in the remaining boat, the *Hattie,* and their reaction to Cataract Canyon
and its rapids was dramatically recorded in their own inscription
at the head of Mile Long Rapid: "Camp #No. 7. Hell to pay. No.
#1 sunk and down." With only one boat for the whole party, they
proceeded cautiously and, like those before them, portaged Satan's Gut.

Best was not the only one to lose boats in Cataract Canyon.
In September 1907, Bert Loper, running with Charles Russell
and Edwin Monett in three steel boats, lost one in the Big Drop.
Like the Best party, Loper's had to crowd into whatever would
float to reach Dandy Crossing, which is now known on the river
as Hite. The following year W.J. Law lost his boat in the Big

Drop, and two years later Pat Malone saw his partner drown in Satan's Gut. In 1910 Satan's Gut claimed two men and a boy. The next year two unidentified men left Green River, only to wreck their boat and perish at the bottom of the Big Drop. Between 1909 and 1912 at least seven men lost their lives in Cataract Canyon.

The challenge of the river as well as the lure of riches have drawn men to Cataract Canyon. Some are known; most are not. But there were some who came and lived to write of their adventures, leaving behind a vivid picture of the Big Drop. On September 12, 1909, Julius F. Stone left Green River, Wyoming, with four boats and the redoubtable river guide Nathaniel T. Galloway. Stone was a serious man with an eye for profit from the fire engines he manufactured in Columbus, Ohio, and the puritan values of mid-America. Unlike the mountain men, the railway builders, or the prospectors, Julius Stone came to Cataract Canyon for pleasure, and he came superbly equipped with four boats built to his specifications and the finest boatman of his day—Than Galloway.

In September the water is low in Cataract Canyon, and Stone found many exposed rocks. One member of the party, S.S. Dubendorff, from Richfield, Utah, careened off the large rock at the top of Mile Long Rapid, lost most of his supplies, and thought he would have drowned were it not for his life jacket. Still, unlike Brown and Stanton, who had lined their boats down the Big Drop in high water, Stone and Galloway were prepared to run. So impressive were the falls that Dubendorff attempted to take a photograph and describe the result: "Wishing the picture of a boat in turbulent water, [Galloway] purposely went through the largest waves of Rapid No. 23 [Satan's Gut] with the result that the boat failed to rise over the second wave; also the third one. Both of these broke entirely over the boat, the first one carrying away the fender and everything else moveable in the boat except myself. The print shows indistinctly the boat just before it disappeared under the second wave, and you see by the result that our experiment was practically barren of the object sought." Still, the first known run of Satan's Gut had been made.

In 1901 Ellsworth and Emery Kolb gazed across the rim of the Grand Canyon and fell in love. The canyon worked its magic, and the Kolb brothers stayed to build a house where they could see in every direction the grandeur of the great chasm. In the next forty years the Kolb brothers ranged through the canyon country, carrying out their profession of photography. They read the report of John Wesley Powell's expedition, and over the years met and talked with Stanton, Stone, Galloway, Russell, and Monett. Year after year they saw the river flowing to the sea and reflected on its many moods, from placid water to turbulent and plunging rapids, visible and, occasionally, audible even from the South Rim. Eventually an idea jelled: why not run the Green and Colorado from Wyoming to Mexico and make the first motion picture of the rapids and the walls that rise above them?

On September 8, 1911, Ellsworth and Emery Kolb left Green River, Wyoming, in two boats, the *Edith* and the *Defiance.* They passed through Red Canyon and Lodore, gaining sufficient experience in Ashley Falls, Disaster Falls, and Triplet to know they should portage Hell's Half Mile. The Kolbs were men of common sense and enormous courage, with a deep love of the canyons, but little river know-how. They pressed on to the confluence of the Green and Colorado and on to the top of Cataract Canyon—by now notorious. Here the Kolb brothers began to feel for the first time the force of water moving through big rapids.

> We always thought we needed a certain amount of thrills to make life sufficiently interesting for us. In a few hours time in the central portion of Cataract Canyon we experienced nearly enough thrills to last us a lifetime. In one or two of the upper canyons we thought we were running rapids, now we were learning what rapids really were.

The Kolbs found more than rapids. Their first night in the canyon they came upon a lone man in an old leaky boat. He called himself Smith. He was dressed in a neat suit and tie, cleanly shaven and if not for the Kolbs would be forgotten. Charles Smith was a trapper who had made his way down the Green River, and although the Kolbs invited him to join them, he was determined to go alone despite his rotting boat and his inexperience. He flipped in the second part of the Big Drop and clung to his capsized boat as it plunged through Satan's Gut. But he survived, still clad in the suit and tie.

Ellsworth and Emery Kolb set out again, running Mile Long and coming to the top of the Big Drop. They studied its first part, watching logs and debris float through. Then they followed, Emery ending on a rock and Ellsworth moving too far to the left only to be pulled back into the main channel by the vagaries of the river, which left him and his boat filled with water. Exhausted, they camped that night on the rocks at the bottom of the second part of the Big Drop and spent the following day reconnoitering Satan's Gut. Then they lined up their heavy wooden boats, as their film shows, and rode the smooth thread between the abysses. On January 18, 1912, the Kolbs reached Needles, California. They had been on the river 101 days.

Charles Smith, the well-dressed trapper, and Galloway, again, passed through the Big Drop later in 1912. Bert Loper and Charles Russell followed in July 1914. From the beginning Loper, a veteran river man, knew they would be in trouble in the Big Drop. Russell's steel boats were only twelve inches deep, and Loper thought they would be sunk in the heavy water of Cataract Canyon.

> The big drop in Cataract Canyon . . . was beyond description. It was a foam, a fury that drowned out even thought. It finished us. My friend lost his nerve and his mind completely. He dropped his oars. His boat swamped.

And Loper's premonitions proved accurate. Russell's boat sank, and so did his own. But the men struggled ashore and then scaled Cataract Canyon's imposing walls. The intense heat blistered Loper's skin, but he recovered his health and his nerve to return to the rivers. Not so Russell, who lost his mind and later

died in a mental hospital. Big Drops can do that to people;
nightmares about whitewater are a milder form of the syndrome.

The pioneering era was over by the time of the First World
War, and recreational river running had not begun. Many who
came to Cataract Canyon did so for business purposes. The year
1921, for instance, found the United States Geological Survey in
the gorge surveying its potential as a dam site and making a
definitive map. Emery Kolb was the head boatman, and in the
manner of trips of this era he personally rowed all the boats
through the biggest rapids. At Satan's Gut, Kolb recorded his experience:

> I ran three boats and had some trouble with each one. Boat one
> hit a rock, whirled bow first, submarined, and an extra oar was
> washed off and gave me a chase to the head of the next rapid
> before it was recovered. Run two an oar lock separated and I
> used an extra paddle to recover it. *Static* also hit a rock but no
> harm was done and we muddled through.

Just another day on the river, but a hard way to make a wage.

Clyde Eddy, however, did not come to Cataract Canyon for
wages. Beaver and gold and railroad routes did not interest him.
His 1927 river trip was the first after Stone's that could be characterized as a recreational adventure. The danger that had re-
pelled earlier river travelers was now a compelling attraction. But
money was not entirely beside the point: Eddy wanted to make a
film of the adventure. He planned the trip with great care. His
boats were twenty-two feet long, had five-foot beams, and were
built of Mexican mahogany with oak ribs. Parley Galloway,
Than's son, was recruited as a guide although he had never been
on the Colorado below its confluence with the Green—the blind
leading the blind. For companions Eddy disdained the seasoned
frontiersmen who had brought Powell down the river and
turned instead to what he called "pink-wristed" college boys.
Eddy had seen them fight in the trenches of World War I, and he
believed in the quality of their character under stress. So, in the
spring of 1927, he placed an advertisement in university newspapers calling for volunteers for an expedition leaving New York

City on June 10 and lasting six to eight weeks. No destination. Eddy wanted to keep his trip a secret so as not to be scooped by a rival filmmaker. In due course the collegians learned they were heading for the graveyard of the Colorado. To buoy spirits, Eddy added a dog, Rags, and a bear cub, promptly named "Cataract," to the expedition. When a bum riding freight cars west stumbled into Eddy's camp at the put-in near Green River, Utah, he, too, became a river runner.

Eddy told the college boys that "successful rapids running calls for intimate knowledge of the river, cool judgment, courage, willingness to take appalling but unavoidable chances, and a fine skill in handling boats." Most of these qualities were not present on the trip. After several flips and the loss of equipment and morale, Eddy's group reassessed its method of operation. Satan's Gut was portaged. Looking at the rapid, Eddy wrote about its "humps" and "pours," but it was the "holes" that scared him most. He wrote:

> "Holes" to me were the most dreadful of the many dangers on the river. Rocks can be seen and they strike you clean and honest blows. Whirlpools are quiet and their dangers lie hidden below the swirling surface of the turbid stream. The possibility of being struck by a falling rock is remote. A "hole" may be hidden anywhere below an innocent looking "hump" in the surface of the water and the churning fury of its vortex—the eddying turmoil of its roaring, foaming water—brings swift death to any man thrown into it. His puny effort is hopeless, struggling vainly against the current which inevitably sweeps him under the "pour," battering him against the rocks until he is dead.

In fact, this has happened, but Eddy's melodrama was undoubtedly a function of his inexperience.

Worn out from the long portages, and more than a little disillusioned about the romance of river adventure, the Eddy party emerged from Cataract Canyon and floated down the comparatively mild Glen Canyon to Lee's Ferry. There five of the crew abandoned ship. The bum, McGregory, continued into the Grand Canyon only to scream in the middle of its first major rapid, "I quit! I quit!" Put ashore in an hysterical condition, he ran for the cliffs and, without a backward glance or his personal possessions, scrambled up a draw and disappeared. But the other travelers, learning by doing, pressed on through the Grand Canyon and ended the trip at Needles, California, August 8, 1927. Although they had swum several rapids, the dog and the bear cub completed the run. A college boy took Rags home, but Eddy rather callously sold the bear cub for $40. Sick of each other and tired of the strain of the river, the group disbanded with no love lost. Yet Eddy could rise above the absurdities and the anger to write of his trip as "an exhilarating voyage into a storyland where dreams are real and the constant pressure of danger gives richness to life." Those words still ring true.

Whitewater rivers seem to attract unusual human beings. Clyde Eddy was certainly one. So were the zany members of the Pathé-Bray motion picture crew that traversed Cataract (portaging Satan's Gut) in the fall of 1927. The next year Glen R. Hyde negotiated the canyon in a scow-like boat steered standing up with sweeps. With him was Bessie, his new bride, and at five feet and ninety pounds she became the first woman to run the Big Drop. She did not, however, emerge from the Grand Canyon, perishing, some say, in an accident around Mile 232 along with her husband. The alternate version of the story has Bessie shooting the cruel Glen, pushing him overboard and climbing out of the gorge to assume a new identity. The scow, at any rate, was found intact and right-side-up, floating in an eddy with no one aboard.

Recently, the story has made the river rounds of a small elderly woman who took a Grand Canyon commercial trip and as the Hyde's story was being told calmly announced that she was Bessie. In the face of disbelief, she supplied unknown details about the trip. Was she worried about being arrested for murder? Not really, she said, because no one would believe her anyway.

The second women to run Satan's Gut were Dr. Elzada Clover, a botanist, and her assistant, Lois Jotter. In 1938 Norman Nevills took them through the canyon on the first kind of trip that would be recognized as a commercial river run in today's terms. The passengers paid $250 for a run from Green River, Utah, down Cataract and Glen canyons and through the Grand. Glen Canyon is, of course, a lake now, but a comparable commercial trip today would cost close to $3,000. In Cataract, Nevills did not prove to be an ideal leader. Although handsome and charming, his nerves and his ego frequently surfaced. At one point his blunt-bowed "cataract" boat drifted away from shore and ran four rapids without an oarsman. The fact that Nevills had considered portaging the same rapids lessened his credibility. At Satan's Gut both Clover and Jotter swam when their boat overturned.

Although not recognized as such at the time, the most prophetic run down the Gut was Amos Burg's in 1938. Burg, who was a photographer of international reputation, presaged the new age of recreational river running by using an inflatable rubber raft. During World War II the inflatable assault craft was refined and improved to attack the Pacific island bastions of the Japanese Empire, and huge quantities were manufactured. Surplus military inflatables began to appear on western rivers shortly after the war. Compared to previous equipment, the inflatable was relatively inexpensive, so its widespread availability represented a key development in the growth of river running as a sport. Inflatables, moreover, bounced off rocks and, with multiple air chambers, they seldom sank. Dick Griffith, Kenny Ross, and Bus Hatch were among the first to use inflatable craft on the Colorado after the war, but the application of this technology to large recreational river trips owes most to Georgie White.

The average person, as she would say, could probably not imagine an individual such as Georgie White. She created a second revolution in river running in the American West. The first revolution had been inaugurated when Than Galloway turned around to face downstream. Every boatman since Galloway has followed this technique, which gives greater control and maneuverability in rapids. The second revolution was precipitated by Georgie White's use of military-surplus inflatable rubber rafts. The neoprene rafts built by the United States Navy were fifteen feet long and seven feet wide. At least on a calm ocean they could float ten men plus equipment. Known as "ten-mans," they were manufactured by the thousands and sold for as little as $50 at the end of the war as surplus. In 1946 Harry Aleson of Rich-field, Utah, bought a smaller "seven-man" inflatable raft, in which he and Georgie White ran Cataract Canyon and Satan's Gut. On that trip they upset in some rapids and portaged around others. From 1947 to 1954 Georgie made several runs through Grand Canyon in a ten-man, sometimes alone. Other-wise, only the odd person or the stray outdoorsman ventured into the canyons during those years. Until he crashed his plane and died in 1949, there was Norman Nevills with his cataract boats, but his trips were expensive (prices rose to $1000 per per-son for the Grand Canyon after the 1938 trial run) and only for the few. For better and for worse, Georgie White changed all that. She opened the river for the many.

It was in 1954, halfway through a trip down the Grand Canyon, that Georgie made an important contribution to the "inflatable revolution." She lashed together three of her ten-man rafts side-by-side, thereby obtaining greater capacity, stability, and safety than any craft previously had offered in the big water of the Colorado. One innovation of the "triple rig," as it soon be-came known, was that it was run perpendicular to the current by two oarsmen manning sweeps in the front and back. But of greater consequence, the triple rig permitted more people to run the river with fewer boatmen and in greater safety than the fragile, hard-hulled boats of Galloway or Nevills. Along with Bus Hatch, Rod Sanderson, and Moki-Mac Ellington, Georgie and her triple rigs led the way through Cataract for later boatmen like Dee Holladay, who has run Satan's Gut more than any other riverman. To this day a properly lashed and loaded triple rig is the most stable rowed boat on big western rivers.

The triple rig was only the beginning. In the winter of 1954 Georgie followed the lead of Blaine Stubblefield up in Hells Canyon purchasing three neoprene bridge pontoons, thirty-seven feet long and shaped like big sausages. When lashed together and steered by an outboard motor, these inflatable pontoons formed a raft twenty-seven feet wide that could carry as many as forty people and surge straight through the biggest rapids on the Colorado. Georgie wanted to introduce her passion for the river country to more people at less cost, and the pontoon raft, with subsequent refinements by commercial outfitters, made it possible for thousands to take the water-level route through the canyons. But ironically, this product of her ingenuity has been a factor in transforming river running from the wilderness experience she knew to mass outdoor recreation with all its attendant problems.

Georgie's most extraordinary run in Cataract Canyon came in 1957, when she encountered the highest water stage since that seen in 1927 by Clyde Eddy, his collegians, the dog, and the bear. The Big Drop was enormous on June 14, 1957, at a flow of at least 100,000 cubic feet per second. The head boatman was Fred Eiseman, who had run the Grand Canyon on two occasions but knew little of the upper river. But he realized, immediately upon entering Cataract, that he was in for a big ride.

As every honest boatman knows, there are moments when the equipment compensates for human error or helplessness. The stability of the triple rig did it for Fred Eiseman in Cataract Canyon that day. The Big Drop was a maelstrom, and it left an indelible impression upon him and his passengers. A passenger, Joel Sayre, wrote:

> Well, Cataract may be absolutely lousy with rocks, but I can't remember seeing a single one sticking above the surface. I remember nothing but waves and waves. They were gathered in conventions and these conventions seemed to stretch from cliff wall to cliff wall, the biggest waves heaped up in the middle, and the smaller ones curling in from the sides to join them, gathering force on the way. And the conventions got larger and tougher to deal with as the run went on.

Twenty years later Fred Eiseman remembered:

> My recollections are of total helplessness. The water was so high and so powerful and fast that there was no doubt whatsoever

who was in charge—the river. I had no feeling of being able to
affect the course of the boat, except when in an eddy. There
were almost no rocks in the river to avoid. If there had been, I
wouldn't have been able to avoid them anyway. As soon as one
shoved the boat off from shore, it was caught in a powerful grip
of the current, and the enormous energy of the water made any
attempt at rowing seem ridiculous. It was about all we could do
to hang on, try to avoid the biggest waves, and marvel at how
fast the scenery was going by, and hope we'd make it to shore
before Boulder Dam.

But most of Eiseman's recollections were blurred by the whitewater blender:

Georgie warned of the Big Drop and Satan's Gut. But Cataract's
rapids vary enormously in proportion to the stream flow. In
1957 it was virtually impossible to distinguish one rapid from another. I think it would have been impossible even with a map
and guidebook. The danger resulted from huge waves—laterals
and tail or convergence waves—not from rocks and holes.
There was little shoreline. It was largely submerged. Trees,
partly under water, lined the banks and one was as likely to get
snagged or ripped up by them as by mid-river rocks. If one
jumped ashore to a rock with the bowline, it was extremely difficult to hold on to the boat. In fact, we left one passenger behind, temporarily, for this very reason. I couldn't possibly tell
which was the Big Drop. There was no clear-cut separation between rapids at all—just enormous waves, tapering into huge
waves, tapering into colossal waves, and then way back to just
enormous. Perhaps it was the rapid in which one of our passengers got thrown out. I managed to haul her back in. It wasn't really heroic. I didn't have anything else to do—or at least
couldn't do anything else. More likely, the Big Drop was the one
in which the super colossal waves pancaked the front boat [of
the triple rig] back on to the rear one.

Georgie White put it more succinctly: "I never saw worsen
than Cataract."

Twelve years later, in 1969, Gaylord Staveley and Fred Eiseman ran the Green and the Colorado Rivers to celebrate the centennial of John Wesley Powell's pathbreaking trip. Having run Lodore and Hell's Half Mile, they left Green River, Utah, with six cataract boats constructed of oak framing and marine plywood and camped at the confluence where Powell slept a century before. On July 19, the Staveley expedition left the confluence and floated down to the beginning of Cataract Canyon, running with precision: Staveley first in the *Norm* and Doug Reiner bringing up the rear in the *Joan*. Unlike those who had gone before, the seven boatman and passengers ran smoothly down the beginning of Cataract Canyon. As they dropped through the Fifth Rapid their thoughts were on the Big Drop that lay below. They ploughed through Mile Long, digging their oars into the crests of great waves and riding out the troughs.

On the left-hand side of the river opposite Teapot Canyon there is a long sand beach behind which are mountains of driftwood. Below the beach is the top of the first stage of the Big Drop. Staveley and Eiseman scouted it, but one of their boats, the *Sandra* was holed by a hidden rock and nearly sank before making shore. The holes in *Sandra* were so large that at first it appeared the boat would join the others at the bottom of this reach of the Colorado. But the crew worked all day, cutting, sawing, and patching with planking, resin, and fiberglass. By evening the *Sandra* was ready for Satan's Gut. Staveley described it:

> The river above was nearly brought to a standstill by [the rocks'] close-set, steeply coursed arrangement from bank to bank. Then, when it finally pitched over the edge, the waiting rocks instantly tore it to shreds.

The rapid seemed unrunnable, but as he continued looking, Staveley saw a ray of hope:

> A strand of water emerges taut and glistening from a chink somewhere up near the brim of the harsh, bouldered face and stretches down to disappear into the featureless turbulence below. It is narrow and it shines and its slippery-smooth appearance sets it visually apart from everything else in the rapid.

Looking down on it is almost like looking into an immense surgical incision. The name of the rapid is apt; its most prominent feature looks visceral. Down that glossy filament of water that was no wider than our boats we'd have to run to make it. Entered right it would amount to perhaps three boat-lengths run between bottomless, thrashing abysses, then safe water below. Entered wrong . . .

Better not to ponder that possibility too long.

On the 1969 trip Staveley ran Satan's Gut, then looked back to see the *Bonnie Anne* move too far to the left, hang on the brink, and drop into the enormous hole. The boat rose up as if trying to escape, but sank back and turned over. There was recovery—there always is on a good expedition—but Satan's Gut had once again flexed its muscles.

Sometimes, to be sure, the rapid wins. In 1983 Cataract Canyon ran a modern-era record high: 107,000 cubic feet per second. Several commercial parties arrived at the top of the Big Drop only to find other groups waiting and wondering. Altogether more than two dozen pontoons, triple-rigs, and dories huddled in what eddy shelter they could as the swollen river roared by. The boatmen stared at Satan's Gut a long time. No one wanted to swim their customers in water so wild. Finally a number of the guides said, in effect, "no más!" This was the 1980s, so instead of walking, radios came out, and helicopters and jet boats arrived soon afterwards to ferry the clients back to their motels in Moab and Green River, Utah. The boatmen returned to run Satan's Gut only after the high water had passed on down to Lake Powell—no point, after all, in taking chances with the anatomy of the devil.

I am a semireligious person. When it sucked me back in the second time I said, "Man, I'm going to die. God, here I come" [but] it was so pitch black I thought I was in hell.

MIKE MAY

Redside

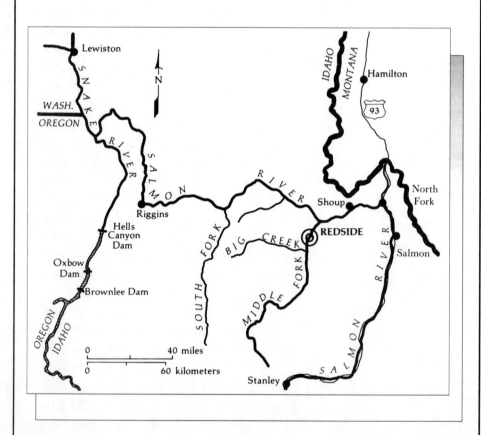

Chapter 6

If there is magic on this planet, it is contained in water.

LOREN EISELEY

The wild canyon of the Middle Fork of the Salmon River lies deep in the high country of Idaho, west of the Continental Divide. Central Idaho remains today the largest wilderness area, outside Alaska, in the United States. Fortunately, much of it is protected as the Frank Church–River of No Return Wilderness. The Middle Fork is one of its major arteries. Isolated and remote, it nestles in the heart of the Salmon River Mountains, a chaotic jumble of peaks and ridges north of the tumultuous crags of the Sawtooth Mountains. So formidable are the approaches that pioneers long avoided the canyon of the Middle Fork. Yet this isolation is now its attraction. Here in the golden summers are brilliant wild flowers scattered through high meadows that disappear into precipitous ravines and deep gorges, the sides of which are covered with tall pines. The peaks and battlements that defend the Middle Fork of the Salmon are crusted with snow most of the year, but in the heart of the canyon, where elk winter, there is little snowfall. In its upper reaches the canyon of the Middle Fork is the home of the lodgepole pine, Douglas fir, and the Engelmann spruce; farther down the canyon appear the western yellow pines, especially along Big Creek, which flows eastward into the Middle Fork from a vast wilderness. Downstream, in Impassable Canyon, are ponderosa pine, mountain mahogany, and, higher up on the slopes, the bitterbrush.

Below the passes of the mountains that defend this wilderness are lakes filled with the crystal water. White men came to the uplands of the Middle Fork in search of gold but found mainly trees and water in liquid and solid form. Occasionally, however, they discovered a bubbling hot spring, an unexpected contrast to the icy waters of the lakes and the creeks that plunge down to meet the river. Through this high country are trails as old as the Indians and the animals they hunted.

There are over forty major rapids from the launch area below Dagger Falls to the confluence with the main Salmon ninety-seven miles downstream. But in the high water of the spring runoff the Middle Fork, with its descent rate of twenty-six feet per mile, becomes one continuous rapid. In June 1974, when flows peaked at 20,900 cubic feet per second, the United States Forest Service described any attempt to run the river as "suicidal." Even in lesser years the upper river is so swift that boatmen have little time to rest on the oars and drift with the flow. The Middle Fork is a millrace punctuated by major rapids. There is Velvet Falls, with its lethal midstream reversal, and Powerhouse Rapids, with its dozens of midstream boulders and a cliff at the bottom. Some boatmen have persistent trouble in Pistol Creek, with its tight S-turn in a narrow channel; there the waves lash powerfully and chaotically back from the perpendicular walls. Farther downriver, Tappan Falls has claimed more than its share of boats. It requires skill and sensitivity to hit the right-hand slot at the top of the falls. Rubber Rapid has twelve-foot waves in high water and also demands precise placement at the entrance. The Redside-Weber complex, however, is a killer.

A Big Drop is unmistakable when you are on the river, but the names people pin on places cause confusion. The Forest Service, the U.S. Geological Survey, local river guides, and out-of-state boatmen all have taken the liberty of applying different

names to the same rapid on the Middle Fork. The rapid at
Golden Creek generally called "Redside" is also known as "Porcupine," "Eagle Rock," and "Sevy's Rock." Just below is a drop
called "Weber" but also called "Redside," "Little Porcupine,"
"Loin of Pork," and "Corkscrew." In high water there is really little differentiation; little chance to pull out. When boatmen think
of Redside they include the rapid just downstream: Weber.

Redside takes its name from the colorful cutthroat trout that
live in the cold, clear waters of the Middle Fork. The rapid has
none of the trout's subtlety, but much of its power and guile. It
lies on a right-hand curve of the river, its entrance guarded by
three huge midstream rocks and the holes below them. At normal water levels the obvious run is right between two of the
rocks, but the drop is sharp and the surging current can spin a
boat unpredictably. Most boatmen swing close to the right-hand
rock to take the drop. Then a hard choice confronts them:
downstream just a few dozen feet is one of the worst rocks on the
Middle Fork. In appearance it looks friendly—round, smooth,
and symmetrical. But the current from both the right- and left-
hand slots slams directly against it. Boatmen have the option of
trying to pull left of this gumdrop-shaped rock in heavy current
or trying for a right-side run. The latter involves precise maneuvering at the top of the rapid. If a boat barely skims the right entrance rock, and if it has enough lateral momentum on the
tongue, it is possible to catch the big eddy behind the rock and
come almost to a stop. From this position making the pull right
of the lower rock is no problem. But in the accelerating current
at the top of the rapid, such a course is much easier plotted than
rowed. For the heavier boats rowed with the ungainly sweeps fa-
vored by Idaho guides, it is almost impossible. The consequence
of missing the eddy is ramming the lower rock. The lucky boats
spin around it, one side or the other; the unfortunate are
pinned against the rock or flipped.

In high water it is possible and necessary to hug the right or
inside bank all the way around the curve at Redside. A giant hole
spans the center of the river, but the rocks that normally block
the far-right chute are sufficiently covered to create a washboard

down which a boat can bump. The lower rock, which in high water becomes submerged and causes a gigantic, churning hole, is kept at least in theory to the left. However, under runoff conditions the water below Redside is the fastest on the Middle Fork. In a matter of seconds, boats that have passed through Redside face the vicious, angled waves of Weber Rapid and serious hydraulics. Indeed, in the minds of many Middle Fork boatmen, "Redside" signifies a full half-mile of whitewater beginning at Golden Creek and continuing past Mist Falls. Historically it has proven the toughest stretch on the river.

Weber is also on a right curve of the Middle Fork. An enormous rock extending from the right bank forces boats down a gauntlet of waves and holes. These increase in size until, at the center of the curve, a vicious hole extends almost the full width of the constricted river. No one really misses this hole. A good run clips its right corner and the jolt is terrific. Less fortunate boats enter farther left, toward the hole's greatest depth. Often boats hit this hole sideways—the result of frantic efforts by the boatmen to pull right. A flip is more than likely in low water and probable in high. And then the worst part: a long, energy-sapping swim in 45-degree water in which one's survival time is just a few minutes.

The character of the Middle Fork has been determined more by those who bypassed its wilderness than by those who attempted to exploit it. Central Idaho has been, and remains, vast, roadless, and primitive. In the 1830s the mountain men employed by William Ashley were roaming through the Snake River country to the south looking for beaver. Others, like John Work of the Hudson's Bay Company, had been there before, but they all stayed far from the great crags which protect the Middle Fork. With few exceptions, the great issues of the American West were decided far from the Middle Fork of the Salmon. The mountain men had adapted to and identified with the Indians, but they moved on when the beaver were gone. The miners were different. They claimed the land and disputed its patronage with the original inhabitants. Gold was discovered on the Clearwater in 1860, and rich strikes followed on the Salmon River, in the Boise

Basin, Coeur d'Alene, and elsewhere in western Idaho. In 1863 a party of miners under the leadership of John Stanley wandered to the source of the Middle Fork where they found bear in profusion fishing for the spawning salmon. And here in Bear Valley, as they named it, the Middle Fork of the Salmon starts on its way to the sea. To the west, in the basin of the Salmon River, mining towns flourished, then died when the gold was exhausted. After the miners came the sheepherders and potato farmers, supported by the railroads which penetrated into the valleys of lower Idaho. In 1863 Idaho itself became a territory. The frontier days were over, but the Middle Fork country remained wild and it still is. As the bumper sticker puts it, "Idaho is what America was." The vast ocean of peaks and ridges are still ruled by elk, deer, mountain goats, and sheep. There are wolves here and a few grizzly and lots of mountain lions.

Like any frontier, the Middle Fork attracted people who were dissatisfied at home, men like Trapper Johnson who, at the end of the nineteenth century, had cabins scattered throughout the mountain country, and others, like Johnny Levine and Ed Chamberlain, who trapped through the canyon for beaver and otter. Cougar Dave was famous throughout Idaho as a mountain lion hunter. He was a remarkable man, not so much because of his accomplishments but because of his eccentricities. His real name was David Lewis, and the remote wilderness around Big Creek was his personal fief, where he roamed with his dogs, hunting and killing, until his death in 1956 at the age of ninety-three. One who knew him said, "His eyes were as cold as the back of a lizard and his skin was as leather thrice tanned, and his walk had the stealth of the cougar itself." Others came to the canyon to homestead on what flat land they could find. There was not much. Jim Bollard and his partner McNerney mined and raised hay and cattle at Thomas Creek; Jim Hash and his wife gardened at Little Creek, downriver; Ray Mahoney cultivated a large orchard at Mahoney Creek; and Bob Ramey and Jack McGivney ranched at Loon Creek. Many failed; those who were attracted to the Middle Fork could be called survivors.

The recorded history of the Middle Fork begins with warfare.

The American Indians had long wandered up from the valleys east and west of the central Idaho wilderness through the canyons and creeks of the Salmon River watershed. Living in isolation, their world of forests and streams was challenged from the outside by hairy men with pale faces. The cultures clashed, and there were heroes and villains on both sides, those who sought to understand and those who did not wish to. The newcomers bypassed the great primitive area of the Middle Fork. They encroached into Indian territory in eastern Washington and Oregon, and in 1878 the Bannock Indian war raged throughout southern Idaho and eastern Oregon. Defeated and in flight, many of the Bannocks drifted up into the wilderness area of the Middle Fork, seeking safety in the mountain fastness populated by the Sheepeater Indians.

The Sheepeaters were actually Shoshone. They had settled in the high uplands at the headwaters of the South and Middle forks of the Salmon River. Living in isolation, these mountain people, numbering about 150, had learned to survive in this demanding land by hunting the mountain sheep from which they were given their English name by the Army that subdued them. Many Bannocks, after their defeat in the war of 1878, chose the hardy but free life of the Sheepeaters rather than reservations.

No one, least of all the United States Army, had shown any interest in the Sheepeaters until 1879, when they were blamed for ambushing four white men in Long Valley and killing some Chinese laborers mining for gold near Oro Grande. Many attributed these attacks to agitation by the defeated Bannocks who had joined the Sheepeaters. The result was one of the most ill-conceived and unnecessary campaigns in the history of the Indian wars. When news of the killings reached Boise, Captain Reuben S. Bernard was directed to lead a detachment of seventy men of the First Cavalry to determine if the murderers were indeed Indians and, if so, to capture them. At the same time a second detachment of mounted riflemen of the Second Infantry left Camp Howard, now Grangeville, Idaho, under First Lieutenant Henry Catley. The two units were to move up into the high country and trap the Sheepeaters in a pincer movement.

Brilliantly conceived in theory, this strategy had no place in what one soldier called "the wildest and most impenetrable region of indescribable ruggedness and grandeur where lofty mountain summits alternate with abysmal canyons." From the outset everything went wrong for the cavalry. Deep snow blocked the valleys; the supply columns could not keep up with the advancing troops, who starved in their camps; and, of course, there were no Indians. The horses perished, the men faltered, and some died of spotted fever. In fact, Captain Bernard's company was so severely debilitated that he suggested recruiting the Umatilla Indians as guides to find the Sheepeaters.

In August, Bernard's column made its way slowly down Big Creek, led this time by Umatilla scouts. The Sheepeaters were there. As the troops moved down Big Creek there was a continuous exchange of rifle fire between the Sheepeaters and the advancing scouts and cavalry. On August 20 the Sheepeaters attacked, were driven back, and hastily dispersed on foot into the high country above Big Creek and the Middle Fork. Bernard pressed after them, but the heavily armed cavalry could not hope to catch the fast-moving Sheepeaters in country they knew intimately. Horses and pack mules went lame, and the cavalrymen, their clothes in tatters, were exhausted. The pursuit was abandoned. By the time they returned to Boise, Bernard's troop had covered 1,200 miles and had lost over 60 animals trying to catch 150 Indians. Finally, in September 1879 the Sheepeaters surrendered—to weariness and hunger rather than to the hapless First Cavalry. Indeed Captain Bernard's most endurable contribution may have been the naming of the gorge below Big Creek "Impassable Canyon." He had horse travel in mind; river runners also find this stretch of the Middle Fork taxing because it contains Redside Rapid.

River running on the Middle Fork developed much later than on the Colorado. No one knows who first ran the Middle Fork, but according to a contemporary Middle Fork boatman and river historian, Cort Conley, Captain Harry Guleke, the redoubtable and famous river man of the main Salmon River may have made the run on a wooden raft about 1925. Guleke commented, "I knew I wouldn't get into a place I couldn't get out of. Sometimes I was on the raft and sometimes I was under it. But I was never afraid. And until a man is afraid, he'll be all right."

Precisely when Guleke made this trip, from what put-in, and why remain unknown, but now men were coming to the Middle Fork not to look for gold, not to trap, nor to homestead, but for the river-running experience. The first to seek it on the Middle Fork were Bus and Alton Hatch of Vernal, Utah. Their river experience began on the nearby Green, and in a strange way owed much to that giant of the previous generation of Vernal boatmen, Nathaniel Galloway. The Hatch brothers were friends of the deputy sheriff of Vernal, Frank Swain. In 1931 Swain brought to prison one Parley Galloway, Than's son, who had been arrested for failure to support his family. The talk turned to river running, and Parley promised to help Swain and the Hatches design a boat if they would cover his bail. They did, but then Galloway left town abruptly. However, the Vernal men had caught the whitewater fever and learned enough to build serviceable whitewater boats of wood. On one of their semi-commercial runs on the Green, they included as a passenger Dr. Russell G. Frazier, a physician at the Kennicott Copper operation in Bingham, Utah. Frazier, who was known as "Big Joe," had one essential contribution to make to exploratory river-running in the Depression years: money. He bankrolled a trip to Idaho, and in July 1935 appeared with the Hatches and Frank Swain in Bear Valley to try the mysterious Middle Fork of the Salmon. It was a low-water year, and the men encountered rocks and fast water rather than the big waves and huge holes of rivers in the Green and Colorado system. After just a few miles the men ran out of patching materials and aborted the run.

Frazier returned the next year, 1936, found higher water and, with Frank Swain and Bus Hatch as boatmen, successfully ran 125 miles from Bear Valley down to the confluence with the Main Salmon. The river was in the doctor's blood, and he returned yet another time, in 1938, to the big-name rapids of the Middle Fork—Velvet Falls, Pistol Creek, Tappan, and Redside— on an expedition sponsored by the *Deseret News* of Salt Lake City.

That year the heaviest snows in a generation covered the Sawtooth Mountains. There was not another runoff like 1938 until the disastrous year of 1970. The flow of melted snow was swollen by heavy rains that turned even the most peaceful creeks into torrents. Undaunted, Russell Frazier and Frank Swain put in on July 4 at Bear Valley in their wooden cataract boats. Hurtling down through fast water, they looked in disbelief at the mounds of debris piled along the banks and across the river by the force of fast-moving water. Within two miles, two of the four boats were destroyed on the rocks, and the expedition itself ended in an hour and a half, with the members walking out of Bear Valley for help from horse packers. At the time, Frazier thought their problems were caused by faulty design of the wooden cataract boats, but the Middle Fork in flood can humble any boat that floats.

After the failure of 1938, Frazier and Swain returned to Utah determined to construct better boats for an expedition down the Middle Fork the following year. They continued to refine their Colorado-born cataract boats for the low water and tight corners of the Middle Fork. The 1939 trip was completed, but the heavy wooden craft still took a fearful pounding from the rocks. However, a new idea came to the river that year. Amos Burg had run the Green and Colorado the year before in an inflatable raft. He brought another one to Bear Valley with Frazier and Swain. Unlike today's inflatables it had a waterproof deck broken only by the rower's cockpit. By all reports Burg found the Middle Fork a piece of cake; he didn't even wet his shoes! This pioneering raft run led the way for the tens of thousands of inflatables that have crowded the river in recent years. Back in Vernal, Utah, Bus Hatch remembered Burg's success and bought several dozen thirty-three-foot inflatable pontoons when they went on sale (for $25!) as military surplus after World War II. This was the start of Hatch River Expeditions, still a leader in western whitewater outfitting.

Another innovation of the 1939 river-running season was the McKenzie River drift boat. Constructed by Woodie Hindman, an Oregon boat-builder, the craft was state-of-the-art for its time. An amazing 400 pounds lighter than the boats Frazier, Hatch, and

Swain used, Hindman relied on quick moves and a low draft to pass through and over rocks. Oregon's McKenzie is very similar in character to the Middle Fork of the Salmon, and Hindman had found the right formula. His only passenger in 1939 was his wife, Ruth. Discounting the Hyde's unfortunate experience in the Grand Canyon eleven years earlier, the Hindman's run at Redside stands as the first of a Big Drop by a married couple. Female boaters today will be interested to know that in 1946 Ruth ran her own boat, an inflatable, down the Middle Fork. By this time Prince Helfrich and other Oregonians had joined Hindman in offering the first of what would become an enormously popular commercial run.

In the late 1950s and early 1960s there arose a sudden interest in America's vanishing wilderness. The backcountry was rapidly disappearing before an expanding and motorized population. There emerged an increasing sense of urgency that portions of the country must be set aside to preserve a wilderness environment for the future. These deep feelings and love for the wilderness, combined with the love of free-flowing water uninhibited by dams and unpolluted by the residues of an industrial society, produced legislation to protect the vanishing wilderness. There were few completely wild watersheds left in the United States. One of them was the Middle Fork.

On October 2, 1968, the Wild and Scenic Rivers Act designated the Middle Fork of the Salmon one of the eight wild rivers initially to be included in the National Wild and Scenic Rivers System. The act defined wild rivers as "those rivers or sections of rivers that are free of impoundments and generally inaccessible, except by trail, with watersheds or shorelines essentially primitive and water unpolluted. These represent vestiges of primitive America." The inclusion of the Middle Fork in the Wild and Scenic Rivers Act brought the river under the management of the Forest Service in an effort to preserve the natural condition of the river and the quality of its uncontaminated water and to protect its environment from development. The trout remain, thanks to barbless hooks and catch-and-release regulations, and the salmon still make their annual migrations. History pervades the canyon, from the remnants of the Sheepeater campaign at Soldier Bar to the cabins of prospectors and homesteaders who sought the sanctity of isolation.

The Frazier-Swain-Hatch trips were expeditions, but by the latter part of the 1960s, particularly after the designation of the Middle Fork as a federally-protected river in 1968, running the classic clearwater stream of the West became first a business and then an industry. In the year of Wild and Scenic designation, about 1600 people floated the Middle Fork; twenty years later the figure was 7,000. A quota system and a lottery allocate demand. About 55% of those who start toward Redside do so in private groups; the remainder use commercial outfitters. But even so your changes of obtaining a private permit in the annual lottery for prime time (July) is one in twenty-five! And if you do "draw out" a permit, your battle with the bureaucracy is not over. At the put-in you must choose campsites for each night of the trip. Big Brother—in the guise of the United States Forest Service—monitors every group's whereabouts on a large chart. Given the limited number of campsites and the fact that seven parties start out each day, this system is not unreasonable. But it smacks of motels rather than wilderness camping. Frazier, Swain, and Hatch would be astonished at what has transpired on their lonely river.

Unlike the Colorado River, the Middle Fork is a truly primitive river—wild, uncontrolled by dams, transformed only by the whims of nature. A free-flowing river like the Middle Fork can change dramatically from one year to the next, depending on the snows and the rains of early summer. Low water exposes the rocks in Redside and Weber and makes for tight runs that are particularly nervewracking to those with hard (as opposed to inflatable) boats. When the river is high, it becomes a writhing white snake. At Redside a wall of water seems to block the entire river.

Even the best boatmen fear the Middle Fork in full flood, and even their judgment can be confounded by the force and power of moving water. Such was the case in 1970. Late snows had fallen on the mountains surrounding the basin of the Middle Fork that year. Just as the snows began to melt, heavy rains poured down the streams and tributaries, flooding their banks and turning the Middle Fork into a raging torrent. On Sunday, June 21, 1970, three parties set out from Dagger Falls to run the river. Before they reached the first bend below Dagger, they all knew they had problems. Everett Spaulding, a veteran boatman from Lewiston, Idaho, had two wooden McKenzie River dories and a sixteen-foot, ten-man raft. Gene Teague rowed one dory and Ken Smith the raft. They were to rendezvous at Indian Creek, thirty miles below Dagger Falls, to complete the party of six, including the NBC news anchorman Tom Brokaw and his friends from the world of business and banking.

A few hours later a second party, led by Alfred E. Couture, an engineer in the Denver office of the United States Bureau of Reclamation, and twelve others, mostly from Denver, left Dagger Falls in two twenty-two-foot rubber pontoon rafts. A short time later a third group, led by Stanford University professor Donald Wilson, departed from Dagger with nineteen people in four ten-man rafts. Fueled by the high water, the Middle Fork became a millrace down which the parties careened in the narrow, congested gorge. The river's power was awesome, the water flowing at ten to fifteen miles per hour through eight to ten-foot waves. In all, forty-three people took to the Middle Fork on that June Sunday. Five days later three of them were dead.

Having reached Indian Creek, Spaulding met the remaining members of his party and continued on to Whitey Cox Hot Springs to fish and bathe in the warm waters not far from the grave, marked by a tangle of elk and deer horns, of the prospector who gave his name to the springs. The night before, Spaulding had confessed with his accustomed reticence that the river from Dagger Falls to Indian Creek was the fastest and most difficult he had ever experienced. Here at Whitey Cox Hot Springs, Couture's party passed Spaulding's and pulled ashore below, deeply concerned by the powerful force of the water and the big rapids which lay ahead downstream. Couture and Spaulding did not know that the third party upstream had already met tragedy. Sulphur Creek meets the Middle Fork just a few miles below

Dagger Falls. Ordinarily a modest stream, Sulphur Creek had become a turbulent tributary. One of the boats in Don Wilson's party had flipped, and Wilson had attempted to swim across the river to assist those stranded on the other side. But the rope to which he had unwisely tied himself straightened in the powerful currents and dragged him under. He was dead by the time he was pulled to shore. Completely demoralized and leaderless, the party broke up, some walking back to Dagger Falls, others continuing with the body down twenty-six miles to Indian Creek and safety.

On Wednesday, June 24, the two remaining parties pressed down the Middle Fork. The water continued to rise, increasing its velocity and the violence of the rapids. That day both parties ran Tappan Falls, Aparejo, and Jack Creek rapids. Couture camped at Wilson Creek, while Spaulding pulled to shore a mile below at Rattlesnake Creek. A few miles beyond, Big Creek was overflowing, adding substantially to the swollen waters of the Middle Fork and the danger of the big rapids just below in Impassable Canyon.

As they raced down river the parties were friendly, but Everett Spaulding clearly disapproved of the Couture party running without a professional guide. Outwardly insignificant, the attitude of the professional guide toward the self-outfitted amateur has since become an issue of great emotion and controversy in running western rivers. As the number of people permitted by government agencies has now been limited and the carrying capacity of rivers has been reached, the spaces allotted to the commercial outfitters and to the rapidly growing number of private runners has produced bitterness, hostility, and even lawsuits, as the private runners seek to gain a greater percentage of the available spaces. With the total number of people fixed, such spaces must, of course, come at the expense of the commercial outfitters. Around the campfires on western rivers the dispute rages. Self-outfitted boaters say their trips are more in keeping with the spirit of a wilderness experience where self-reliance should be emphasized, and the trip is earned rather than paid for. Commercial outfitters argue that not only is river running their livelihood, but their experience and knowledge of the river enables them to provide a safer trip than the noncommercial runner. But, Redside Rapid on June 25, 1970, did not prove to be convincing evidence for the case of the commercial outfitters. When the Spaulding party left Rattlesnake Camp, only about half wore life jackets.

Reaching the confluence of Big Creek and the Middle Fork, the river runners started to enter Impassable Canyon. Porcupine Rapids had big waves, but Redside was worse, and a hundred yards beyond Redside were the huge waves of Weber Rapid. On that Thursday Alfred Couture liked nothing he saw at Redside. "At the head of the rapids lay an enormous hole that spelled almost sure disaster if we pulled into it. The river was curving to the right so the force of the current drove our boats to the left."

Couture studied the three slots of Redside Rapid and watched the river sweep down the center tongue to crash into and over the huge boulder at the bottom. With limited maneuverability in his twenty-two-foot pontoons, Couture had little choice but to run center where the full force of the flood waters were being drawn to the big boulder and its hole like a magnet.

I put all my strength into the oars to avoid that treacherous hole, but I didn't quite succeed. We went down into it about 10 feet from the center, rose to the top, and hung there for a moment that seemed endless, suspended at the very crest of the wave with the river frothing around us. I had experienced that same sensation once before, at Lava Falls in Grand Canyon; a split second later we had overturned on that earlier trip.

But we were luckier this time. The pause was short-lived, and then we shot downstream again.

Plunging on through the enormous waves of Weber Rapid below Redside, Couture's rafts were big enough to negotiate the waves, but so swift and powerful was the current that they careened on down Impassable Canyon virtually out of control. They swept past Parrot Place Camp, where despite the best efforts of the oarsmen they could not land. Down the river the pontoons hurtled, running rapid after rapid as the boatmen frantically tried to land. Not until Cradle Creek Camp were they able to work the pontoons into an eddy to pause in their flight, only to see a life jacket with its lifeless body sweep past in the current and spin into Ouzel Rapid below.

Everett Spaulding had run Redside down the center and pulled his dory into an eddy below to wait for Gene Teague who was going to line his boat. Teague completed lining his boat and began to move downstream under oar power again. The supply raft followed, hitting the center of Redside and, like Couture, clipping the hole. Tom Brokaw, who was in the raft, has graphically described the next horrible moments:

The craft creaked and groaned. For a moment the wall of water was all there was to see and hear. In another instant, the wave retreated and we were safely through.

I looked up to see Teague, with Stone and Harmon as passengers, heading into Weber Falls . . . .

Suddenly I noticed that Teague's boat appeared to be stalled in the middle of Weber Falls.

It was sinking.

Later, Stone described the scene. He said a huge wave broke above them and practically filled the right side of the boat.

Teague yelled out, "Shift your weight, shift your weight," and he began frantically pulling on the oars, trying to move to calmer waters.

But it was too late. Another wave rolled over the other side. All three men were swept into the raging, ice-cold water. . . .

Downstream I could see Stone and Harmon neck deep in the middle of the river, racing in tandem toward another set of rapids. Teague was off to the side and behind them heading for the same rapids.

Suddenly we had our own problems. The raft flipped over when hit by a powerful wave as it plunged into Weber Falls. As I tumbled into the water I was stunned by the ferocity of the current. In a lifetime of swimming I can't recall a greater struggle to break back through the surface, even with the assistance of a life jacket.

Scrambling on top of the overturned raft, Brokaw and his friends did not linger, but leaped as one into the water and swam to shore and safety. The others downstream were not so fortunate. Brokaw continues:

For Stone, Harmon, and Gene Teague, it was a battle of survival. When they first were washed from the boat Stone knew they were in trouble. Even with a life jacket he could barely keep his head above water as strong, deep currents insisted he join them.

Harmon, recalling Spaulding's advice, pulled himself onto the hull of the overturned boat when it surfaced. He saw the bow line trailing in the water near Stone and yelled, "Grab the line, get the line."

By pulling himself up on the rope, Stone was able to look around. He saw a small eddy off to the right. His impulse was to swim for it and he shouted the question to Harmon, "Do you want to try for shore?"

"No," Harmon yelled back. "Hang onto the boat."

Stone's impulse continued.

"Let's swim for it."

This time, from behind him, Teague yelled, "No, stick with the boat, hang onto the boat."

Stone was impressed with Teague's calm. He was wearing a life jacket and holding a seat cushion, looking as serene as a Sunday stroller. That was the last Stone saw of Teague, ever. The water quickly became much rougher, and although he couldn't see more than a few feet downstream, Stone was certain they were moving into rapids again.

He was right.

He started into the rapids trailing Harmon and the hull of the boat, straining to hang onto the rope as he was sucked under water, battered by currents on every side, fighting for the surface and another breath. When he did break free, Stone still had the rope, but he was a few feet in front of Harmon who was still on the battered hull. They didn't speak, concentrating only on their private struggles for aid.

Harmon was taking wave after wave flush in the face as they washed over the hull, and the numbing effect of the 40-degree water was weakening his grip on the boat, as it was Stone's on the rope.

Stone's will also was beginning to weaken.

"This is a dream. I'm not even supposed to be here. I'm supposed to be on the raft. I'm gonna die," he thought.

Just then he was sucked under water again and the rope was torn from his hands.

When he struggled to the surface for what seemed like the hundredth time, Harmon and the boat were gone.

He had no choice. He had to swim for shore. Near death from exhaustion alone, Stone flailed against the surface currents, convinced that he was making no progress. And his tennis shoes, incredibly heavy, were dragging him down.

But gradually the water was less turbulent. Ahead of him he could make out the calm surface of an eddy.

Mustering his remaining strength, he churned out of the current and into the eddy. Totally spent, he draped himself over a boulder in shallow water, afraid he'd collapse and drown if he tried to make the final, few steps to shore.

Below Weber the remains of Spaulding's party set up a makeshift camp while Spaulding, who had successfully run Weber, pressed downriver alone looking for the lost men. At Cradle Creek Camp he came upon the Couture party, and together they continued down through a series of rapids in the last seven miles to the confluence with the main Salmon. The rest of the party was taken out by helicopters the following morning. Ellis Harmon's body was found three miles below the confluence. The river never gave up Gene Teague. In the words of Everett Spaulding: "That river swallows people. Some it gives up; some it don't."

News of the disaster spread quickly on the river "telegraph." Upstream two parties aborted before reaching Redside and Weber. Frank Gifford, the football hero, and Sir Edmund Hillary, first up Everest, were among those who left the river. Perhaps they knew that big drops care nothing for reputations.

Big Mallard

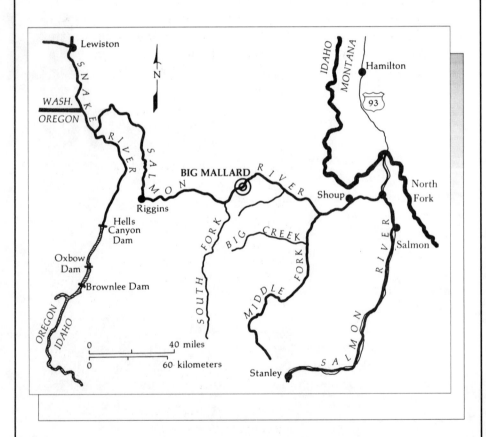

Chapter 7

What use are rapids?
What use are we if we remain indifferent to challenge?
What are we worth if we won't feel exhilaration?

DAVID BROWER,
JEFFREY INGRAM,
MARTIN LITTON

Having raced over a hundred miles from the upland meadows around Bear Creek, the roiling waters of the Middle Fork abruptly end in a placid confluence with the mainstream Salmon—the fabled River of No Return. The Salmon was born millions of years ago when a rising mass of granite known as a batholith uplifted the great wilderness region of central Idaho, buckling the crust of the earth into a chaos of mountains and canyons.

The waters which had flowed eastward, ultimately to the Atlantic, now poured out of the Sawtooth and Lemhi valleys down through the Salmon River canyon to the Snake, the Columbia, and the Pacific Ocean. The snows of the Sawtooth, White Cloud, and Bitterroot mountains feed the river as it flows 425 miles across Idaho, draining a basin of 14,000 square miles and dropping from an elevation of 8,000 feet to 905 feet where the Salmon meets the Snake. Beginning west of Galena Summit, the Salmon is a small mountain stream you can step across. It flows north, absorbs the waters of hundreds of tributaries, then turns dramatically to the west into the canyons of no return.

Technically the canyon of the Salmon is the second deepest gorge in the North American continent—deeper even than the Grand Canyon and surpassed only by Hells Canyon of the Snake—but the crests of the mountain ranges lie far back from the river and do not rival the continuous mile-high rims of the Grand Canyon. Between the river and the peaks is a land of immeasurable beauty: blue lakes, deep forests, and alpine meadows through which bubble clear-flowing brooks.

With the Middle Fork adding to its muscle, the Salmon becomes a big, powerful river that drops twelve feet per mile from the North Fork to the Wind River Bridge not far from Riggins, Idaho. The combination of major as well as minor tributaries and a continuous drop has produced over forty rapids, well-known to rivermen by such names as Pine Creek, Salmon Falls, and Gunbarrel. At high-water flows, above 65,000 cfs, Ruby, Whiplash, and The Slide are the trouble spots. Big Mallard, in fact, washes out. But at low and normal flows, and with reference to river history, Big Mallard has a well-deserved formidable reputation.

The rapid is dominated by two huge boulders situated close together on the left side of the Salmon. A narrow, twisting slot exists between them, and at all but the lowest water levels that seemingly improbably route is the one to take. From the top of the rapid, at the point of the big curve, it looks tempting to go right of the big rocks. But a boulder bar protruding somewhat illogically from the right, or outside, of the bend forces the river left. Boatmen have positioned themselves far right—at the edge of the bar—pulled right with everything they have for two hundred yards and still been swept directly into the monster hole behind the left-hand rock.

So Big Mallard is generally scouted. The boatmen pull in on the left bank above the curve. There all is quiet, for the thick woods that crowd to the river's edge block the view and thunder of the rapid as the river swings out of sight. It is an eerie feeling, for the boatmen know the rapid is there, but they cannot see or hear it. They pull their boats into the deep quiet pools by the bank. Interspersed among the rocks and pines are bunch grass and currant bushes in blossom. On the slopes and meadows above the river are yellow bell, sagebrush, and buttercups tucked among the trees. Above, golden eagles with talons locked tumble in play or sex downward through thousands of feet of crystalline air.

The boatmen see this, but they are not at Big Mallard to watch eagles. They are there to hit the slot between the two boulders, so they stumble through the rocks along the bank, slipping and cursing, around the curve. There they sit or stand and stare, watching the Salmon rushing through the slot.

The conclusion that boatmen reach is to run the rapid on the left—tight around the curve, straight down the bank, and directly toward the two lower holes. This is careful calculation, not insanity. A close reading of the rapid reveals a tongue of smooth water, about three yards wide, racing between the gaping holes. Hit that tongue, and it is one of the cleanest, most satisfying whitewater runs in the West. Miss it by only a few feet, and it is one of the wettest.

Sweeping toward the tongue from upstream, a boatman's confidence tends to fail. The tongue itself is not visible. To the right and left he sees enormous mounds of water and, in low water, the rocks. Beyond that is space and the river far below the rapid. Adding to his problem are tricky waves along the left bank that kick the boat off its line. Corrective maneuvers must be delicate so close to the shoreline rocks. Strike one and the boat would spin out sideways, and there is no room for a boat in that position on Big Mallard's tongue. Finally, about thirty feet above the chaotic holes, the tongue appears: a sliver of smooth, green water laced through the white. There is time for a few corrective strokes before a properly aligned boat slices through the turbulence. Bouncing down the tailwaves, the same thought occurs to everyone: "Did you see that *hole!*" Some call it "China Hole," presumably because it seems deep enough to reach that nation on the other side of the world.

The Big Mallard country has had a long and dramatic history of Indians, missionaries, miners, mountain men, and rivermen. The Shoshone Indians called the Salmon "Big Fish Water," for its trout, steelhead, and huge salmon. They told Meriwether Lewis and Captain William Clark that it was a river of no return, unnavigable by their canoes. Acting on the orders of President Thomas Jefferson, the explorers had started out from St. Louis in the spring of 1804 to seek the fabled Northwest Passage to the Pacific through the newly acquired Louisiana Purchase. Crossing the Continental Divide, they camped on the Lemhi River, a tributary of the Salmon, where (Clark wrote) the Shoshone chief, Cameahwait,

> ... placed a number of heaps of sand on each side which he informed me represented the vast mountains of rock eternally covered with snow through which the river passed. That the perpendicular and even jutting rocks so closely hemmed in the river that there was no possibility of passing along the shore; that the bed of the river was obstructed by sharp pointed rock and the rapidity of the stream such that the whole surface of the river was beat into perfect foam as far as the eye could reach. That the mountains were also inaccessible to man or horse.

Dismayed that Cameahwait's information "fell far short of my expectations," Captain Clark nevertheless continued down the Salmon to just above the present settlement of Shoup. Here Clark turned back. Remembering Clark and Lewis were the sort of writers who could spell a word three different ways on one page, read Clark's journal entry for August 23, 1805:

> The River from the place I left my party to this Creek is almost one continued rapid, five very considerable rapids the passage of either with Canoes is entirely impossible, as the water is Confined between huge Rocks & the Current beating from one against another for Some distance below . . . my guide and maney other Indians tell me that the Mountains Close and is a perpendicular Clift on each Side, and Continues for a great distance and that the water runs with great violence from one rock to the other on each Side foaming & roreing thro rocks in every direction, So as to render the passage of anything impossible.

The natives added that bigger rapids were common further

down the river. Convinced that the Salmon could not be their route to the Pacific, Lewis and Clark returned to make their way over Lost Trail Pass *back* across the Continental Divide, and then via Lolo Pass across the divide one more time to the Clearwater River and the Columbia. The canyon of the Salmon, which in the words of an old-timer many years later, "seems like the Creator chopped it out with a hatchet," remained unvisited. But in retrospect, and considering how much Lewis and Clark suffered on the Lolo Trail, perhaps they should not have given up on the Salmon so soon. Its waters were the most direct route to their destination: the Pacific Ocean at the mouth of the Columbia. Sure there would have been portages, but they were makeable. And even if a boat or log raft had to be abandoned, there was no shortage of trees with which to build a replacement. If Lewis and Clark had been just a little more confident about whitewater, if their river experience had not been shaped by the placid Missouri, if they had had Powell's persistence, their pathbreaking journey to the Pacific might have been substantially easier . . . or at least different.

The first white men to float the Salmon were Hudson's Bay Company trappers associated with John Work's Snake River Expedition of 1832. It must have been a bit brisk on March 26 when L. Boisdnt, A. Dumaris, H. Plante, and J. Laurin started down the river in a skin canoe. The wilderness swallowed them. The next news appears in John Work's journal for July 19. After making their way down the Salmon for thirty days, Plante and Dumaris had drowned. The survivors, who lost all their gear with the canoe, eventually made their way with the help of Indians to Fort Nez Perce. They arrived, so the story goes, stark naked. What they thought of Big Mallard was not recorded.

Mormons entered the Salmon River country in the 1850s and established a mission for the Indians on a tributary they called "Lemhi" after a character in their holy book. They constructed a fort, farmed, and preached to the Bannock and Shoshone Indians. Life was hard on the Lemhi. Crops were decimated by grasshoppers, and the providential seagulls did not arrive to save the day. To sustain the mission, supplies had to be hauled from Salt Lake City, four hundred miles to the south. In fact, the great distance from Salt Lake brought criticism from Brigham Young himself. In 1857 when he visited the post, he told the missionaries they had gone too far from the Mormon heartland, and he preached in a sermon upon his return to Salt Lake City about the probable failure of the mission. Nevertheless, he renewed his efforts to keep the Lemhi mission intact by sending sixty more missionaries to bolster the original group of settlers. By the autumn of 1857 over a hundred Mormons were actively working to turn Lemhi into a substantial Mormon community.

Although well-intentioned, the missionaries were not particularly successful in converting the Bannock and Shoshone. After some initial conversions they found the Indians unwilling to abandon their traditional ways for those of the Mormon. Dissension within the community over the harsh living conditions at Fort Lemhi only exacerbated the frustrations of the missionaries at their failure to convert large numbers of Indians. Moreover, relations between the missionaries and the mountain men who trapped in the Salmon River country had become increasingly strained. Mountaineers have traditionally not been enthusiastic for religion, and the arrival of the Mormons appeared to threaten the trade with the Indians. Indeed, the growth of the settlement disturbed the Indian and mountain man alike, for the coming of farmers threatened the manner of life and livelihood of both. Supposedly incited by the mountaineers, the Bannock and Shoshone Indians attacked Fort Lemhi, driving off the stock and killing two Mormons. Brigham Young closed the mission, and the Salmon River country returned briefly to the Bannock, Shoshone, the Nez Perce, and a handful of mountain men. But the times were changing, and within three years men motivated not by God but by gold were pouring into the Salmon River valley and its tributaries.

For some decades before the first big strike at Pierce, it was common knowledge that there was gold in the streams of Idaho. Father De Smet, an early pioneer Catholic priest, reported its presence in the 1840s, and French Canadians discovered a small

site in 1852 on the Pend d'Oreille River. There were other ru-
mors of gold, but it was not until 1859, when Captain E.D. Pierce
discovered gold in Canal Creek near Orofino, that the rush
began. By 1861 word had spread of Pierce's find, and in August
there were seven thousand men and women in what was called
Pierce City. From Pierce the miners swarmed up the creeks and
valleys looking for the precious metal, and mining camps sprang
up at Orofino, Elk City, and ultimately in the Salmon River country. Right behind the miners came the traders who supplied
them with food, equipment, whiskey, and women. By the autumn of 1861 a tent city of some ten thousand inhabitants had
spread out at the head of Baboon Gulch, which was renamed
Florence. The miners kept working into the winter, but as the
snow piled deep in the uplands the town found itself completely
isolated until May. Food prices soared, and many became ill and
debilitated from surviving on flour and pine bark. But the lure
of plentiful gold was too great to discourage the miners. Some
were making $100 a day by panning in the streams, while the ma-
chinery of the placers sucked up the metal from the tributaries
of the Salmon. Others were taking out gold valued at $400 a day
with box-shaped rockers operated by hand. Boom times, bonanza economics! By 1863, however, the inevitable "bust" closed
the camps.

Beginning in the 1870s the Salmon became increasingly used
as a highway through the roadless wilderness. One result was the
appearance of very capable boatmen. Perhaps the best was
Johnny McKay. After his youthful bride was caught in a mill that
he had built and crushed to death, McKay sought solace on the
river. Year after year, beginning in 1872, he appeared in Salmon
City in the spring and built a wooden, flat-bottomed scow ma-
neuvered by sweeps—the kind of watercraft Lewis and Clark
could have utilized. The scow carried McKay down the river
where he would pan enough gold to buy supplies for the next
year's run. A handsome man with a white, handlebar mustache,
McKay traveled alone on the Salmon and the Snake as far as
Lewiston, Idaho. Sometimes he would winter over where gold
and game were plentiful. In almost a half century after 1872,

McKay ran the Salmon more than twenty times. It was a remarkable achievement. By comparison, it was not until the 1960s and
the era of outfitted trips for tourists that any one boatman ran
the Colorado in the Grand Canyon more than a half dozen
times.

   The other giant of early Salmon River whitewater boating was
Harry Guleke. A large, strong man with a booming yet friendly
voice, "Cap" Guleke made his first run on the Salmon down to
Riggins, Idaho, in 1896. Johnny McKay was a veteran by then,
and it is easy to imagine the two boatmen talking about the
rapids. And given the large and clumsy character of the scows
they used, Big Mallard must have figured prominently in their
discussions. Guleke always regarded that rapid as his greatest
challenge. He never failed to scout the narrow slot between the
boulders. In his words, "we always go ahead here and look out."

   Cap Guleke was not in the river running business for fun.
Neither did he cater to tourists, although on occasion a few went
along for the ride for $1000 a trip. What he really did was trans-
port materials—heavy equipment intended to get gold out of
the Salmon River's gravels. The Painter Mine, for example, required transportation of 90,000 pounds of machinery plus coffee, dynamite, sugar, flour, tobacco, and bacon. Guleke's scows
were designed to be workhorses of the river. The so-called
"sweep boats" were roughly thirty-five feet long and eight feet
wide—just enough to squeeze down the slot at Big Mallard. The
boats were steered with two twenty-five foot sweeps the last ten
feet of which was an enormous blade. Although McKay had a
smaller one he could handle alone, controlling a sweep boat
usually required two men—one on each huge oar. Needless to
say, they had to work in a coordinated manner, much like the operators of the front and rear oars on triple-rigs today. Guleke's favorite teammate was David Sandiland, a wiry, quiet Scot whose
younger brother George drowned in the Salmon's Pine Creek
Rapids in 1897 when the sweep he was operating caught on a
rock and catapulted him into the river and under the boat. The
scows Guleke used could carry enormous loads (jeeps and
trucks were not uncommon) but drew only about fourteen

inches of water. They were hard to stop once they got moving, but they had one big advantage: at the end of a run they could be dismantled and sold as lumber. Of course, the river sometimes did the dismantling before the take-out!

One of the most interesting accounts of a Guleke trip comes from the pen of Caroline Lockhart, a novelist with a crush on one of the principals in a Salmon River mine. In 1911 Lockhart was a passenger on a scow captained by Guleke. Dave Sandiland was on the rear sweep. Pine Creek Rapids scared Caroline who envisioned the scow splintering on a rock "like a flimsy strawberry box." But Guleke snaked the boat through and assured his passenger that "It gets worse as you go further down." When she asked for details, he responded: "Yes, there's the Growler, the Big Mallard and the Whiplash that I mind more than Pine Creek Rapids . . . Dave hates the Big Mallard."

When Caroline Lockhart reached the top of Big Mallard and walked down the shoreline with the crew, she made no effort to conceal her terror. What she was about to do seemed to her "the wildest boat ride in America." And, she added, "It is no disgrace to be scared at the Big Mallard. In fact I wish to say that the person who is not afraid at certain places in the Salmon River has not sense enough to be afraid." As the crew scouted the rapid, Lockhart noticed the "grave faces" of Sandiland and Guleke; the swamper or assistant boatman, who had been cocky upstream was "white as paper to his ears." Guleke said that a right run was out of the question with the ungainly scow; they would have to run the slot. Lockhart wrote:

> I could not believe he was in earnest. I had not thought they had even considered this narrow passageway. The space was not wider than twice the width of the boat and the masses of rock so close to the surface on one side, that yawning hole on the other, the turn around the ledge giving so little time to act and get results in the tremendous current that it looked like deliberate suicide.

Lockhart reported that no one spoke as they walked back to the

boat. Her "feet dragged and I had a curious goneness in the region of my belt buckle." The life preserver seemed ridiculously
small. She thought of walking but in the end "crawled limply
into the boat." There was no question in her mind that she was
going to die.

Guleke inched out into the current, "measuring distances
and calculating the result of each stroke like a good billiard
player." Everyone knew that they were playing for more than
they could afford to lose; the stakes of this game were ultimate
ones. The scow floated around the point, close to the left shoreline, and Lockhart noticed a transformation in Guleke. "The
wind blew his hair straight back and the joy of battle was gleaming in his eyes . . . his face was alight with exultation." Like boatmen today, Guleke lived for the Big Drops. They tested his skill;
accentuated his achievement. He may have been just making a
living, but the reason he was doing it on the Salmon was because
of moments like the one Lockhart observed.

"Fearlessness is contagious," Lockhart wrote, and she was
filled with a "spirit of reckless indifference" as they rocketed
down the shoreline toward the slot. It was too late for nervous-
ness anyway; might as well go for the gusto.

The "final rush" lasted only a few seconds. Guleke hit the "to-
boggan slide of water" perfectly. "The boat shot past the rocks on
the left and cut the hole on the right so close that half the stern
hung over it." The assistant boatman was poised directly above it,
and he "stared into its dark depths with bulging eyes."

Of course the odds sometimes caught up with Guleke. Over
the years he lost several sweep boats in Big Mallard. On one
memorable occasion beavers chewed through his tie-up lines in
camp (or at least that's what he reported; oftentimes faulty knots
are the real beavers!) and his boat drifted into Big Mallard without a crew. Almost miraculously, it hit most of the slot, crashing
into one rock and spinning off—damaged but right side up.

By all reports Cap Guleke was a charming man. He would
toss oranges and candy to the children who lived in the ranches
and small towns along the Salmon. He continued to float into
the 1930s when he was over seventy. The final voyage down his

personal river of no return occurred in 1944, fittingly in Salmon, Idaho.

Over the years Big Mallard was the scene of more than one river fracas. An amusing one occurred in 1930. Floyd Dale, a horseman from Oklahoma, had bought what is known today as Whitewater Ranch. The easiest way to get 10,000 board feet of lumber to the place seemed to him down the river. With the help of Charlie Guffel, Dale tied the lumber into a raft. All went well until, in the words of Robert Bailey, "those treacherous Big Mallard rapids, where the veteran pilot Captain Guleke has several times met misfortune." Dale's raft did not make the slot; perhaps it was too large. Slamming the right-hand boulder, the raft started to break up into individual boards. Guffel abandoned ship and struggled to shore. Dale took a little more time, removing his shoes and socks. But when he dove overboard "a giant hand seemed to be holding him back. Try as he would he couldn't shake the giant's hold. Over and over he rolled in the white-capped, rock-strewn waters, but somehow he always seemed to remain near the surface and couldn't sink." Eventually the explanation appeared. One of the spikes that Dale had used to make the raft was protruding from a board and had caught in the seat of his pants. Unintentionally, Dale had provided himself with a novel life preserver. "The Mallard rapids are wicked," Bailey remarked, "and it would have been a miracle for anyone loose among the timber of the broken-up raft to have survived death or serious injury."

A new era began in Salmon River whitewater boating in 1936. Bus Hatch and Frank Swain, Utah boatmen who also made exploratory trips on the Middle Fork of the Salmon, brought their fourteen-foot wooden boats to Salmon City. No one had tried to run the river in small craft before, but they had a successful trip. Their only problems occurred at Big Mallard. In the calm water above the rapid they spotted a black bear and her cub eating berries. They thought they might catch the cub. Distracted, they floated around the curve and suddenly found themselves bearing down on a Big Drop. There was no chance to stop and scout. The first two boats in the party flipped. Hatch watched from upriver and when he tried to run down to assist flipped as well. The fourth boatman, amply warned, managed to begin a right ferry early enough to miss the holes. Finally reunited, the party could count one broken leg, one head stuck in a five-gallon pitch bucket, and an escaped bear cub.

Bert Loper followed the Hatch-Swain group down the Salmon in 1936—also in a small, rowed boat. Then came World War II and widespread availability of aluminum and superior outboard motors. In the late 1940s Clyde and Don Smith and Paul Filer began to build light boats of the new material and found that the outboards permitted them to run upstream. Now a return could be made on the river. Sportsmen and supplies could come up the river from Riggins as well as down from Salmon City and North Fork. To make the job easier, the power-boaters dynamited several boulders out of Dried Meat Rapid, a short but rock-choked drop below Big Mallard. At the time, the deed was cause for local celebration. By creating a channel through which the big boats could roar, the explosives marked one more step in man's conquest of nature.

Inexplicably, Filer and Smith did not attempt to defuse Big Mallard as they had Dried Meat. That rapid remained dangerous for boatmen, whether propelled by power or oars. Filer remembered that his closest call came there. He was following Smith upriver, attempting to hit the same slot between the rocks that the raftsmen seek. The moment of truth was over in seconds, and though Filer had made the run frequently without a problem this time the river made him pay. As he shot into the slot, his boat suddenly broached, slipped sideways, and crashed into the center rock. The impact tossed Filer into the river and his boat began to sink. With Smith above Big Mallard, there was no immediate rescue; and Filer bounced, half drowned, from rock to rock in the lower rapid. Finally Smith realized he was alone, spun his boat, and shot back downstream through the slot to pick up his companion. "I thought I was a goner," Filer admitted. Later he turned philosophical: "You can't fight this river, she'll beat you every time."

In recent decades commercial and private recreational boat-

ing on the Salmon has boomed. The new gold is white and liquid, and people pay big money to mine for memories. Each summer thousands shriek and laugh through the rapids that turned
back Lewis and Clark. At Big Mallard, however, the smiles disappear just as Caroline Lockhart noted. Ahead is the serious business of threading a rocky needle with boat and two oars. It's
sometimes easier for a boatman to get to Heaven.

Granite
Creek

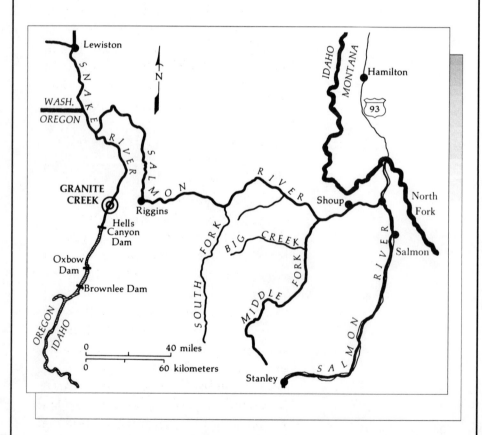

Chapter 8

A river is more than an amenity, it is a treasure.

OLIVER WENDELL
HOLMES

By any standard, one of the most unlikely first descents ever made of a Big Drop was the steamboat *Shoshone*'s successful navigation in 1870 of Granite Creek Rapid in Hells Canyon of the Snake River. This great gorge, which defines the Oregon-Idaho border for over one hundred miles and averages 6,500 feet vertically from rim to river, presented a formidable barrier to river travelers from the earliest days of westward exploration, but the dream of using the Snake as a commercial highway from the interior to Columbia River ports persisted. In 1866 the Oregon Steam Navigation Company built a triple-decked, stern-wheeled steamboat on the Snake some distance upstream from Hells Canyon.

The *Shoshone* was nearly one hundred thirty-six feet long, twenty-seven feet wide, but drew only twenty inches of water. She was fully outfitted to supply the needs of southern Idaho's mining camps. Business, however, diminished with the gold, and the big boat never carried a payload down the Snake. Finally, in 1870 its owners dispatched veteran Columbia River steamboat captain Sebastian "Bas" Miller and engineer Dan Buchanan with instructions to bring the

Shoshone through Hells Canyon and down to the Columbia or wreck it trying. Miller knew what he was about on rivers. He waited for the high, rock-covering water of April to start his run, and he chose to float downstream with his engines in reverse to slow his speed and provide steerage. This was the same concept Than Galloway applied two decades later to smaller, oar-powered boats on the Colorado.

The trip began inauspiciously. The cumbersome steamboat spun out and backed over one rapid, smashing against rocks that shortened its bow by eight feet. Repairs required only a day, but a rolling log struck Miller, knocking him unconscious for another day. Once back on the river, the steamboat somehow survived the big rapids of upper Hells Canyon. At Granite Creek Rapid the *Shoshone* took a terrific pounding. Too wide to run either of Granite's tongues, the huge boat wallowed right through the center hole. Bridging the Snake's huge waves rather than rising and falling with them, the *Shoshone* was torn and wrenched. Planks broke loose; the safety valve came open and steam shrieked. Down in the engine room, Buchanan found himself alternately slammed against one wall and then the other. His steady stream of profanities flew up the speaking tube to Miller who was wrestling with the wheel. But after the rapid was passed Buchanan yelled, "I say, Buc, I expect if this company wanted a couple of men to take a steamboat through hell, they would send for you and me."

When Miller and Buchanan tied up a few days later at Lewiston, Idaho, the townspeople could not believe their eyes. In one of the rapids in Hells Canyon, a plank bearing the boat's name had torn loose and floated downstream. Retrieved from the lower Snake, it seemed conclusive evidence that the *Shoshone* would never be seen again. A memorial service was already being planned when Miller and Buchanan steamed around the bend.

Cleaving the high country of western Idaho and eastern Oregon on its way to the Columbia and the Pacific, the Snake River has cut, in Hells Canyon, the deepest gorge in the American West. Statistically, if not in terms of drama, it surpasses even the Grand Canyon of Arizona. The Snake has an elevation of 1,300 feet in the approximate middle of Hells Canyon. On the Idaho side of the gorge the Seven Devil Mountains rise to a maximum height of 9,393 feet, and the western or Oregon rim has isolated peaks in the Wallowa Mountains attaining 10,000 feet. It is these high points that give Hells its "deepest gorge" reputation, but some qualification should be made in view of the Grand Canyon's mile-high rims extending continuously over two hundred miles.

One of the first Europeans to see Hell's Canyon, Robert Stuart, noted in 1812 how the river "enters the mountains, which become gradually higher. . . . The whole body of the river does not exceed forty yards in width, and is confined between precipices of astonishing height." Although he did not run the river, Stuart also observed how "cascades and rapids succeed each other, almost without intermission." The fury of this water, the blackness of the basalt and granite lining the inner gorge, and the stifling heat of summer combined in time to pin the name "Hells" on the Snake's handiwork.

The canyon has indeed been hell for explorers and travelers for a century and a half. "The state border," one old timer remarked, "is the only thing that runs through that gorge without getting drowned." Although the Snake is logically the best route west from the Continental Divide, the ruggedness of Hells Canyon prevented its development as a transportation corridor like the Missouri or the Ohio. Lewis and Clark avoided it in 1805. Wilson Price Hunt and Donald McKenzie, leading John Jacob Astor's transcontinental expedition in 1811, lost boats and boatmen in the upper Snake, then almost perished traversing the country east of Hells Canyon on foot. Captain Benjamin L.E. Bonneville could not penetrate the gorge on his way to Oregon in 1833. Setting a precedent for subsequent travelers, Bonneville left the Snake at Farewell Bend and struck out across the dry, rough country of eastern Oregon on his way to the lower Columbia and the valley of the Willamette. The Oregon Trail followed this route, and the engineers responsible for Interstate 80N made the same sensible decision a century later.

To this day Hells Canyon remains roadless and railless but

not, unfortunately, without dams. Before 1967, when Hells Canyon Dam drowned the upper reaches of the gorge, the Snake was a strong contender for producing some of the toughest whitewater in the West. In a stretch of fifteen miles there were as many difficult rapids as in any comparable distance in the Grand Canyon, say Hance through Crystal. Some whitewater veterans rated them harder than those in northern Arizona.

In the predam Hells Canyon the first of the fearsome rapids occurred at Kinney Creek. It had a runnable tongue but huge waves in the high water that seasonally boomed down the Snake. Les Jones, the pioneer mapper of western rivers, rated Kinney a seven on a scale of difficulty extending to ten. A mile and a half downstream, Squaw Creek confronted river runners with an extremely sharp initial drop and then yards of rocks. Squaw drew a rating of nine from Jones, and so did Buck Creek Rapid, a mile farther down. Buck was widely regarded as the toughest rapid in Hells Canyon by those fortunate enough to run it before it died under a reservoir. Its drop was an incredible twenty-two feet in fifty yards, and there was no easy way around an awesome hole in the center with a backwave that could toss boats like toothpicks. A photograph from the 1950s of Buck Creek Rapid shows a pontoon raft, about thirty feet long, totally airborne and upside down, equipment and bodies raining from the boat into the rapid. Only a mile after Buck, early Snake River boatmen faced Sawpit Rapid. Les Jones compared it to Hance Rapid, a boulder-choked monster in the Grand Canyon and gave it an eight on his rating scale.

Hells Canyon Dam is the concrete tombstone of Kinney, Squaw, Buck, and Sawpit and the former location of Copper Ledge Falls that gave the early steamboaters fits. But the final two major rapids in the sequence remain. Wild Sheep comes first, five miles below the dam. At 55,000 cubic feet per second, a flow the Snake still regularly attains, Wild Sheep is a strong candidate for a Big Drop. But two more river miles bring boats to the most difficult remaining rapid in Hells Canyon, high flow or low: Granite Creek.

The name as well as the run of Granite Creek Rapid presents

a problem. There is indeed a Granite Creek entering Hells Canyon, and it is a beautiful trout stream, but it is not the location of the rapid that bears its name. Granite Creek drains a major watershed on the Idaho side of the canyon, including the heart of the Seven Devil Mountains. It is a major tributary with an impressive canyon of its own, but this means that in its lower reaches Granite Creek is a relatively mature watercourse characterized by a mild angle of descent. Big rocks, the kind that cause big rapids, do not move readily down such a drainage. Only a small riffle marks the confluence of Granite Creek and the Snake. Passing it, first-time river runners have been lulled into a false sense of security by assuming that the notorious Granite Creek Rapid is really nothing at all.

A half mile farther the real Granite Creek waits in ambush. It is actually located below and caused by Cache Creek, which has all the credentials for making a Big Drop. Cache's drainage is very short and very steep on the Oregon side of the Snake. Black and Bear mountains, both over 6,800 feet, are only two lateral miles up the side canyon. That works out to a rate of descent of something over two thousand feet per mile! Given the flow produced by sudden heavy storms, Cache Creek can move rocks the size of houses and tons of smaller boulders. Such a storm may occur only once in a hundred years, but the Snake has been very patient. The result is apparent to people who read the land. A long grassy terrace, criss-crossed with game trails, hangs a full fifty feet above the confluence of Cache Creek and the Snake. Big rocks have thundered down Cache through the terrace and into the river to form the Big Drop.

Although it is possible to scout the illogically named Granite Creek Rapid from the terrace below Cache Creek, boatmen usually land on the Idaho side of the Snake and walk a horse trail to a vantage several hundred feet above the whitewater. For people who hold oars rather than reins, the view is not comforting. Large rocks, and correspondingly large holes, guard the sides of the river, preventing boats from sneaking down the shoreline. The center of the Snake is a seething cauldron, fully thirty feet across, and below it the water reverses, moves back upstream

138   THE BIG DROPS

against the flow. An enormous rock, brought down by Cache Creek, explains the cauldron.

To the right and left of the big rock are smooth tongues that would seem to offer an easy passage through Granite Creek. But they are very deceptive. Unusually angled waves can funnel boats directly into the seething center pit. An error of only a foot or two in the positioning of a raft almost guarantees an upset. In that case there are three hundred yards of very rough water (rocks in low flows) to swim through. The terror of being upset in Granite Creek is the possibility of being trapped, held, and drowned in the giant hole.

Granite Creek is tough enough at its rocky, low-flow stage, when the left tongue can be followed into a narrow slot between exposed rocks and the center hole. In medium flows the tongues are as steep as any found on western rivers. At high water, which on the Snake means 35,000 to 70,000 cubic feet per second (and occasionally over 100,000), a right-side run is mandatory, and the waves are enormous. Few boatmen dare the Snake at the highest flows.

There is some question about when Granite Creek was first run. In 1862 a Lewiston, Idaho, newspaper published an account of a boat trip up and down the Snake River through Hells Canyon. According to the story, the three men in the party ran every rapid and returned to town glowing with enthusiasm and predicting a golden age of river trade on the Snake. But the 1862 trip is suspect in several particulars. The reported distances between locations along the Snake are so inaccurate (by hundreds of miles) that they throw into doubt the credibility of the reporters. Furthermore, the alleged 1862 conquerors of Hells Canyon state that they "found nothing in the river to impede navigation." If that was their conclusion after actually running the rapids from Kinney Creek to Granite Creek, the three men were either the best boatmen or the best liars in the Pacific Northwest.

It would appear, then, that the voyage of the *Shoshone* in 1870 stands as the first proven run of Hells Canyon and Granite Creek Rapid. The difficulties Miller and Buchanan encountered might have scared off even the most daring, but the hope of steamboating Hells Canyon died hard. Twenty-five years after the *Shoshone*'s wild caper, the *Norma* challenged the Snake. Considered in relation to a rocky, powerful river that narrows in places to 60 feet, the *Norma*'s dimensions are astonishing: overall length, 185 feet; width, 35 feet; deckhouse, 120 feet; cabin deck, 80 feet; pilothouse, 12 feet.

The *Norma*'s run began May 17, 1895. Anticipating trouble, the crew sealed off the boat's multiple bulkheads and filled the front compartments with cordwood to buffer collisions. Despite these efforts one rock ripped a hole in the hull 40 feet long. The crew at this point made clear their reluctance to continue the trip, and reluctance turned to near rebellion when a ferry operator reported that he had seen "a drift log a hundred feet long up end and go under one cliff and it never came up."

Captain W.P. Gray had a problem on his hands. In the tradition of Christopher Columbus, he dealt with it by assuring the men he would turn back shortly, all the while knowing that once committed to the current of Hells Canyon there was only one way out. So the *Norma* pressed on, racing down channels only a few yards wider than her hull. On the steep tongue of Granite Creek she nosed down so sharply that her stern paddle wheel came completely out of the water to spin wildly in the air. A member of the crew reported that "Captain Gray stood at the wheel, apparently as calm as though shooting Hells Canyon was an everyday occurrence. His confidence," he added, "gave us all courage, and we watched, fascinated with the wild scene, our hearts pounding against our ribs as each new danger approached and quickly passed." Years later Gray wrote that on the Snake "I had no chart or pilot but found my way by reading the character of swift water which has been my vocation since as a boy thirteen years old I handled canoes and batteau on the Fraser River."

On May 24 the *Norma* docked at Lewiston, the many stove pipes jammed as caulking in holes in her hull giving the appearance of a gunboat. There was good reason to be proud. Never before or since has so large a boat successfully run such difficult

rapids anywhere in the world. However, the final victory belonged to the river: the *Norma*'s run marked the end of the
steamboat era in Hells Canyon.

After the *Norma*'s 1895 effort, runs of Hells Canyon were few
and far between. A railroad survey crew navigated the gorge in
1911 but lined almost all of its big rapids after breaking a boat in
half the first day out. Another group of surveyors carried their
boat around Granite Creek Rapid in January 1920, only to have
the unsettling experience of travelling through the lower canyon
as part of an ice flow that blanketed the river from shore to
shore. These were the last people to give serious consideration to
using the Snake for freighting. Only one economic bonanza remained untapped. The same wilderness and whitewater that
broke the dreams of empire builders enticed recreational river
runners. The future of boating in Hells Canyon would belong to
those who coveted rather than cursed the rapids. In due course,
companies outfitting vacationing tourists would wring more
money out of the Snake than all the early miners, trappers,
steamboaters, and railroad builders combined.

The era of running for fun on the Snake in Hells Canyon
began in 1925 when the remarkable Amos Burg showed up
above the gorge in his whitewater canoe *Song O' the Winds* which
he rowed rather than paddled. Burg was twenty-four with mati-
nee-idol looks, a penchant for style (he sometimes wore a jacket
and tie on river trips), and an unsatiable craving for moving
water. For example, Burg's 1925 trip began at the source of the
Snake River south of Yellowstone National Park. On earlier adventures he had paddled the Inside Passage off British
Columbia's coast, twice floated the Columbia River from its
source to salt water and followed the Yellowstone, Missouri, and
Mississippi all the way to New Orleans. He would go on to become the most widely-traveled river runner of his age and a
member of the prestigious Explorers Club. Burg set a pattern for
modern adventurers who try to finance their addiction for
wilderness with photo-journalism.

In 1925 young Burg joined forces with John Mullins, a local
prospector, who claimed to know every rock in Hells Canyon.

Burg later joked that his familiarity must have come from hitting them all! The men lined the biggest drops in the canyon including, in all probability, Granite Creek. After the most difficult water was passed, Mullins caught a horse and rode out of the gorge. Burg, characteristically, continued down the Snake to the Columbia and all the way to Portland.

In subsequent years Amos Burg canoed the Inside Passage from Alaska to Portland, Oregon, ran the Yukon, Slave, and Athabaska Rivers, and sailed a twenty-six foot boat around South America. We have met him before in an inflatable boat on the Middle Fork of the Salmon in 1939 and will later find him in the Grand Canyon. As for Hells Canyon, Burg ran it again in 1929 and 1946. On the latter trip he ran Granite Creek. Burg's final trip on the Snake was in 1978 when he was seventy-seven. The best of Hells Canyon whitewater was under a reservoir by this time, but Burg really had few grounds for complaint. He had danced to river music when it was wild, free, and lonely to a degree present-day floaters can only envy.

In the early days sometimes years passed with nobody running, or even seeing, Granite Creek. Then a boatman, looking small and fragile, would appear on the trail over the rapid and stare into its colossal hole. Such was Robert J. Wood, the postmaster of Weiser, Idaho. In 1939 he became sufficiently curious about the canyon he lived near that he decided to float the Snake with five friends. They scouted Granite Creek's two tongues in an effort, Wood stated, to pick "the lesser of two evils." After much deliberation, Oren McMullen, who weighed 230 pounds, started his run with two passengers while Wood watched from shore. As the current above the rapid quickened, the powerful McMullen rowed so hard that he broke one oarlock and lost his hold on the other oar. It was low water, and the huge center rock loomed directly ahead. For Wood, on shore, "seconds seemed like hours." Then:

> The prow of the boat rose as she stood on end as the water hit the rock. Mac grabbed the tow rope as it dropped past him. Pledger fell off into the water. Parker grabbed a hand rope and

hung on—put his foot out and the next second Pledger grabbed it and before you could say it, he had his arms around Parker's neck. [The boat] stood on end—how long I do not know. I do know that two still cameras [on the shore] set and ready to push the button were forgotten entirely . . . and . . . the crucial moment remains unrecorded. Finally, a backwash brought the boat to an even keel and it slowly backed up into the stream and on down the river. We all drew a sigh of relief.

It was several miles and two more, smaller rapids, however, before the oarless boat could be dragged by swimmers to the shore.

In July 1940 two reporters from the Lewiston *Morning Tribune* made the first detailed record of a run of Granite Creek Rapid. Clarence Moore and Paul Jones used two wooden, oar-powered boats, named *Snake Charmer* and *Hells Belle.* John Olney, a local Oregon boatman, led the party. Also on the trip was Kyle Mc-Grady, who had begun to win a reputation as an operator of the motor-powered mail boat that served the ranches below Hells Canyon.

Putting their boats on the river a few miles below Homestead, Oregon, the Olney party proceeded cautiously. They lined Kinney Creek Rapid and portaged or lined the next three big ones: Squaw, Buck, and Sawpit. The first night's camp was at Deep Creek, just below the present site of Hells Canyon Dam. Early the next day they encountered a rapid where, according to Moore, "The water . . . poured over a large rock and then plunged directly toward the river bottom." This was Granite Creek.

John Olney, rowing the first boat, proceeded into the whitewater, got thrashed, but somehow made it through upright. Seeing Olney's boat bobbing in the tailwaves, Moore and McGrady slid down the right-side tongue.

Seaworthy as our boat was it could not stand being pushed upward on one side and sucked down on the other. It flipped over so quickly that I was still in a sitting position when I tumbled out, head first and bottom up. An undercurrent caught the three of us . . . and swept us under the river. It must have been

more than fifteen feet [deep] because my ears ached from the
pressure for about six hours. I recall the changing current turning me about in the water in slow motion as some "amazing stories" report that men do in mythical space ships, and all the
time I was wondering if I was apt to hit any rocks.

Moore finally surfaced in the tailwaves, still beneath his overturned boat. Almost unconscious from lack of air, he barely extricated himself and floated to shore. Yet he had the river in his
blood; his final statement in the newspaper was a vow that he
would make "another trip tomorrow if I could."

The reputation of the big rapids of Hells Canyon attracted
the nation's best river runners. In 1946 Norman Nevills trailered
his pie-shaped "cataract" boats from the canyons of the Colorado
to those of the Snake. His trip included the first women to run
Granite Creek. In the early 1950s Blaine Stubblefield became the
first boatman to offer regular commercial float trips in Hells
Canyon. After experimenting with hard boats, "Stub" went over
to rubber in 1951. The three thirty-three-foot pontoons he
lashed together and powered by an outboard motor were ungainly, but they had the decided advantage of being hard to flip.
Old photographs show Stubblefield's rigs being folded nearly in
half by the huge waves of Buck and Granite Creek Rapids. From
1954 to 1958 Georgie White brought her version of a multi-
hulled, inflatable whitewater boat to the Snake. Her "triple rigs"
utilized smaller rafts than Stubblefield's although she later
adapted the big bridge pontoons to the Grand Canyon. Don
Harris and Jack Brennan also made multiple commercial runs of
Hells in the 1950s with sixteen-foot, oar-powered hard boats. In
1957 Les Jones concluded the pioneering era, in a sense, by
making a detailed scroll map of the river and a guide to its
rapids. To his credit Jones changed the erroneous label "Granite
Creek Rapids" to "Cache Creek Rapid," but the correction made
no headway against custom and tradition. The name of the Big
Drop remains "Granite Creek" to the continuing confusion of
the uninitiated.

The post-war years also found Kyle McGrady, the garage mechanic who had flipped in Granite Creek on the John Olney trip, pushing his fifty-eight-foot powerboat farther and farther up Hells Canyon. McGrady's philosophy of river running was simple and forthright: "You gotta keep lettin' that river know who's boss or you're a goner sure." But he never tested his method against Granite Creek, electing to run only the lower portions of Hells Canyon. The first powerboatman to run Granite Creek from the bottom up was Bob Smith of North Fork, Idaho. In 1952 Smith climbed Granite's staircase in an open aluminum craft powered by two thirty-five-horsepower outboard engines. Smith also ran up through Buck, Sawpit, and the other predam monsters. The feat remained one of the most impressive in the history of boating on the Snake until 1962 when Smith and Paul Filer blasted up and down Hells Canyon in a twenty-four-foot aluminum boat with 100 horsepower.

A major river like the Snake magnetizes dam builders. In 1941 a group of engineers ran Hells Canyon on a business trip. Asked by reporters if they had experienced any "thrills" on the trip, their spokesman coolly replied, "We were impressed by the rapids rather than thrilled." What did thrill the engineers was the abundance of dam sites in the canyon. In the ensuing years some in the upper gorge were utilized for Brownlee Dam (1958), Oxbow Dam (1961), and Hells Canyon Dam (1967). Drowned under reservoirs were most of the original Big Drops of Hells Canyon. Indeed, only eighty-five miles of free-flowing river remained after the dam builders finished their work. Then, seizing on a Federal Power Commission recommendation that more dams in Hells be authorized, utility companies made plans to complete the taming of the Snake. Granite Creek Rapid would have gone the way of Buck, Kinney, Copper Ledge, and the others. But a 1967 Supreme Court decision, spearheaded by a longtime friend of wilderness, Justice William O. Douglas, forced reconsideration. The Court simply asked if the Federal Power Commission had considered the option of building no more dams at all on the Snake and sent the case back for further study.

The 1967 decision encouraged friends of a wild Snake. Citizen conservationists brought forward the fact that no less than eighteen dams already impeded the river's flow. Of the Snake's entire thousand-mile course only the eighty-five miles below Hells Canyon Dam and a few miles in Wyoming remained free-flowing. This was becoming a matter of concern to more and more people, among them Senator Robert Packwood of Oregon. On April 14, 1971, he addressed the United States Senate on the subject of saving Hells Canyon. A few weeks later Packwood ran the river. At Granite Creek Rapid he became so excited that he kayaked the next five miles under the tutelage of Walt Blackadar.

With the status of Hells Canyon becoming a major national environmental issue, more politicians wished to see firsthand what all the fuss was about. On August 14, 1972, three United States congressmen arrived at the top of Granite Creek Rapid with Jim Campbell, a commercial river trip outfitter. Already nervous because of the congressmen's presence, Campbell's boatmen paled when they walked up the horse trail to scout Granite Creek. The Snake's flow was about 14,000 cubic feet per second, and at that level Granite's tongues were extraordinarily steep and narrow. Normally the boatmen would have opted for the left side, but they were anxious to give the congressmen an exciting ride. They would go for it. Cort Conley was running the lead boat, and his positioning was perfect. His twenty-seven-foot pontoon slipped between boiling holes on either side of the right tongue. Conley later admitted, however, "It was the steepest tongue I've ever dropped off in a boat."

As he bucked through Granite's tailwaves it occurred to Conley that if the following boats missed their entry into the rapid by as little as a yard on either side, they would flip. He had no time to land and run back along the shore with his warning, and the roar of the rapid prevented shouting. He could only watch in horror as the second pontoon dipped down the tongue, caught an edge in a hole, and turned bottom side up.

The unfortunate boatman climbed on top of his inverted raft and looked frantically for his passengers. Spotting Congressman James Kee, who was elderly and in poor health, he hauled him onto the overturned boat. Meanwhile Jim Campbell brought the third and last raft down the rapid with no special trouble. Rowing furiously, Campbell caught up with the flipped pontoon and seized its bow line. Then began the struggle to land both boats before the next rapid, already audible downstream. Annette Tussing, reporting for the Lewiston *Morning Tribune*, recorded the moment:

> Rowing with extreme effort Jim [Campbell] finally fell from his seat amidships in exhaustion.
>
> Congressman Mike McCormack, D-Wash., who had been taking his turn at the oars in milder rapids upstream, leaped to the oars now, bracing almost horizontal as he strained to pull the big raft swinging at the end of the ropes, out of the fierce grip of the fast current and toward shore.
>
> Almost there he gave out and James Olson grabbed the oars, also extending himself with unbelievable stamina to move both rafts.
>
> If we missed a small jut of rocks just downstream both craft would be swept into the next rapids.
>
> We were only two feet from the rocks when our raft began losing ground, slowly sliding back toward the ponderous pull of the big craft.
>
> McCormack and Campbell leaped into the deep water bounding the abrupt jut of boulders. Both of them clawing at the smooth slippery boulders, lost holds and slid under our raft, briefly.
>
> Olson still pulled at the oars to prevent us from sliding away from shore again.
>
> Finally, scrambling and clawing, the men in the water got the bowline around a rock. It gave way. Another, and it loosened and tumbled out of place.
>
> A third rock held. The rest of us scrambled ashore on the huge rocks, to help pull the big raft in and tether it to the jumble of boulders which pitched sharply into the deep water.

After a number of deep breaths the party unloaded and righted the flipped pontoon. Congressman Patrick T. Caffery of Louisiana poured water out of the suitcase he had ill-advisedly brought on the river. Several members of the U.S. Army Corps of Engineers along on the trip observed almost in unison that if more dams were built on the Snake such things would not happen. Congressman McCormack replied that the opportunity to challenge, and maybe lose to, a rapid was precisely its value for an increasingly overcivilized society. Yahoo!

A few hours behind the congressional party the same August day in 1972, Verne Huser and Hank Miller had charge of another Jim Campbell trip. They had just finished scouting Granite Creek Rapid when a member of the congressional trip panted up the horse trail with news of the upset. The messenger was supposed to tell Huser and Miller not to try the right-hand tongue, but something was lost in the translation and the boatmen headed directly for the trouble spot. Not wishing to create anxiety among their passengers, they had kept the news of the upset to themselves. But Huser felt considerable apprehension as he drifted toward the roar of Granite in his twenty-five-foot pontoon. Just before the tongue he reminded himself that he had run Granite successfully on ten previous occasions. "I know how to run it," he thought. "Hit the haystack at a slight angle to the right so the angular wave will set us up for the tail waves—no sweat." As it turned out there was plenty!

"Somehow," Huser remembers, "I misjudged the angle and hit the haystack too straight so that the angular wave turned us to the left and instead of riding lightly over the wave, we were at the perfect angle to ride up onto the long curler and be driven right back into that horrendous hole. I had my left oar in the water, and the force of the rollback drove us down into the hole so hard that the oar, which was twelve feet long, hit the bottom of the river and broke in two." Huser believes that before breaking, the oar acted like a brace, keeping the boat upright long enough to wallow out of the hole. He also credits getting out to his boat's low center of gravity, the result of carrying fully packed provision boxes. Perhaps Granite Creek, having already eaten one boat that day, was temporarily satiated.

At the time of the congressional river trip in 1972, the future of Granite Creek Rapid and the remaining wild stretch of Hells

Canyon was undecided. But the pressure of environmentalists and the changing mood of the nation were inexorable. On December 31, 1975, President Gerald R. Ford signed into law a bill adding 101 miles of the Snake to the National Wild and Scenic Rivers System. The same act created a 650,000-acre Hells Canyon National Recreation Area and, within it, a 193,000-acre addition to the National Wilderness Preservation System. Many Big Drops on the Snake have been stilled, but in Granite Creek's case the nation opted to let one remain dancing and alive—a roaring symbol of the old Hells Canyon.

Whitewater oarsmen . . . have given up seats in the California legislature and careers at E.F. Hutton to row you down the wild and mighty rivers. . . Envy them their tans. Respect their skills. And when they come over to your house, lock up the food and beer, and don't introduce them to your sister.

VIRGINIA MORELL

Crystal

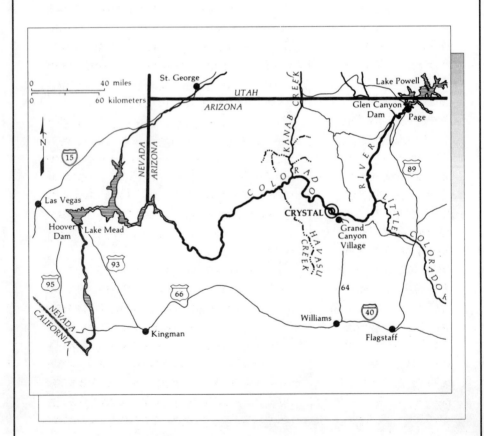

Chapter 9

The great tailwaves were all that anyone remembered of that run, grand, glassy mountains of water with swooping valleys between them; climbing for three boatlengths or more until it seemed we'd lost all power to climb; perching then on a crest as sharp as an alp and wondering whether we'd pitch forward into the next trough or back down the slope onto another boat (everyone saying later they looked up and saw the whole bottom of the next boat out of the water above them on the crest ahead); pitching down into another trough nearly as deep and soaring up to another crest nearly

Rain began to fall over northern Arizona in the grey morning hours of December 4, 1966. An unseasonal, but extremely intense, low pressure system drew saturated air from the Gulf of California and the Pacific Ocean north and east toward the snow-dusted Kaibab Plateau. As the warmer air from the sea rose over the nine thousand-foot Kaibab, it cooled and condensed as precipitation. Such winter storms over the Grand Canyon are common, but this one was different: *fourteen inches* of water fell in a period of only thirty-six hours. One consequence was the almost instantaneous creation of a Big Drop. Earth scientists and meteorologists speak of fifty- and one-hundred-year storms and floods. They mean a phenomenon that only occurs on an average of once every fifty or one hundred years.

The storm of December 4 and 5, 1966, over the Crystal Creek drainage is given at least a one-thousand-year rating. There are no historical records of comparable precipitation for the plateaus north of the Grand Canyon. Indian ruins known to date from the twelfth century and located over forty feet above normal water level in the creek were car-

as high, and after four or five crests finally being sure we would carry over the next, not fall back. And looking around at each other when we reached the still water, almost amazed to see all boats right side up: it was supposed to work that way, but it still seemed incredible.

GAYLORD STAVELEY

ried away by the high waters of December 1966.

In December the north rim of the Grand Canyon is one of the more isolated places in the American West. The road that carries summer tourists forty-five miles from U.S. 89A to the lodge at Bright Angel Point closes after the first snow. Thereafter only the rare snowmobiler or cross-country skier winds through the pines and the aspen and traverses the meadows to stare into the abyss. Almost certainly the great rain of 1966 fell unobserved, but we can imagine it hammering the frozen ground, then quickly collecting in rivulets and moving southward into the canyon. This seemingly obvious fact merits some attention. Had the big rain fallen above the south rim of the Grand Canyon on the Coconino Plateau, there would be no Big Drop at Mile 98.25 on the Colorado River. The slope of the land on the south rim is, somewhat illogically, away from the canyon. The explanation is that the ancestral Colorado River cut through the uplifted northern part of Arizona south of its highest point. The Kaibab Plateau is a full two thousand feet higher than the Coconino. Water runs into the canyon on the north side and away from it on the south.

The Crystal Creek drainage is one of the longest north of the central section of the Grand Canyon. The December 1966 runoff began at Lower Little Park, twenty-five air miles from the Colorado. At the eight-thousand-foot level the water dropped over the north rim. The Colorado was almost six thousand feet below, and in the course of winding toward it, Crystal Creek gathered the waters of a dozen major side streams. But a rainfall that covered every square foot with fourteen inches of water turned each fold in the canyon walls into a torrent. By the time Crystal Creek curled past a long, twisting ridge known as the Dragon and descended into the vast Hindu Amphitheater, it was a raging brown beast. At this point Dragon Creek, almost as long as Crystal, joins it from the east. The combined flow must have been awesome. Powered by a steep rate of descent, lower Crystal Creek moved thousands of tons of gravel and small rock at speeds close to fifty miles per hour. Boulders three feet in diameter were *suspended* in the flow. Larger ones rolled along the stream bed with a low, ominous rumble. Occasional earth slippages and mud flows gave the swollen stream the viscosity of molasses.

Lashing from wall to wall like an enraged serpent, Crystal finally powered into the Colorado. The rocky delta of Crystal Creek quadrupled in size. That pushed the Colorado southward toward Slate Creek, which enters on a fault line directly opposite Crystal. Steep cliffs downstream from Slate constricted the river, forcing it to rampage through the new obstacle course.

The old Crystal Rapid had a moderate drop of about fifteen feet, and the few sizeable rocks in the rapid could be easily avoided in low water. At higher flows there were regular waves of unremarkable size for the Grand Canyon. Not one of the early accounts of running the Colorado even mentions Crystal Rapid. Why should they? In the preceding ten miles the pioneer river parties had to deal with extraordinary rapids such as Horn Creek, Granite, and Hermit; by comparison the old Crystal seemed easy indeed. After December 1966, however, no one ignored Crystal. Overnight it became one of the most dreaded rapids in the West, and, if anything, it has worsened over the subsequent years. Today, particularly at high water, boatmen regard Crystal rather than Lava Falls as the crux run in the Grand Canyon.

   Although no one saw the transformation of Crystal Rapid into a Big Drop, what took place there has been deduced from documented events in the Bright Angel Creek drainage a dozen miles to the east. Bright Angel also begins on the Kaibab Plateau above eight-thousand feet, and its watershed received approximately the same amount of precipitation in the 1966 storm. Dan Doherty, the manager of Phantom Ranch, was living on Bright Angel at the time. Located a mile from the Colorado, Phantom has served hikers and riders since early in the century. Normally it is a cottonwood-shaded oasis. Bright Angel Creek, usually a little hop-across stream, gurgles along below the guest cottages. Doherty recalled the change caused by the torrential rains. The flood struck Phantom Ranch "with the noise of a dozen locomotives."

   Immediately marooned by the rising water, the few persons at the ranch began to fear for their lives, and the mules bolted so high on the canyon walls they later had to be assisted down with ropes. Doherty recalled that the ground trembled under his feet—the result of boulders bounding down the creek bed. "It wasn't just the size of the flood," Doherty remembered, "but the duration of it. It rose up and didn't drop an inch for three days."

   Among the casualties were scores of 150-year-old cottonwoods, stone walls, buildings, irrigation works, and the sewer system of the ranch. One bunkhouse ended up in Lake Mead, two hundred miles down the Colorado. The greatest loss along Bright Angel, however was the brand new water pipeline that ran from Roaring Springs, high on the north wall, down the creek, across the Colorado, and up to the tourist facilities on the south rim. The project cost $2 million, and it was an engineering marvel. In a few hours the creek ripped out the work of two years. Pipe, bridges, and sections of the new North Kaibab Trail disappeared down the Colorado. As mute evidence of the cause, a rock measuring three feet by two feet by two feet was found in the flood's aftermath poised on one of the few remaining bridges, a full thirty feet above the normal level of the creek. It had been carried like a grain of sand in the raging water.

   National Park officer Frank Betts saw Bright Angel Canyon soon after the flood. He also noted the hundreds of cubic yards of raw earth ripped from the canyon walls and the devastation of the Bright Angel delta at its confluence with the Colorado. In Betts' view, "It looked as if the whole Colorado River had come down Bright Angel Creek." The topography showed the result. The trail and pipeline were not reopened for four long, expensive years.

The discharge of Bright Angel Creek did not create a major rapid in the Colorado but rather a series of sharp, swinging bends peppered with gravel bars. It was a totally different story ten miles downstream. The principal way the great flood of 1966 altered Crystal Rapid was by doubling its drop. The outwash from Crystal Creek literally dammed the Colorado with a fifteen-foot layer of rock and gravel. Some of the rocks, particularly those that lodged against the left, or southern bank, were enormous. At high water they cause holes as large as any in the Grand Canyon.

The flood of 1966 narrowed the width of the Colorado passing down and around the Crystal Creek debris fan to one-quarter of its width above the rapid. This constriction increased flow speed dramatically, and when the fast water passed over a large boulder the compression increased. The river needed to dissipate energy. The result was what hydrologists call a "hydraulic jump." River runners referred to it as the "Old Hole" or the "Big Hole" in Crystal—and they usually tacked on a few adjectives unsuited for prime-time viewing! The hole-wave combination seemed twenty feet high, but no one quibbled about specifics. One look at the seething cauldron and the steep black wall of water, and you knew it was something you *really* wanted to avoid.

Change is the only constant on rivers, and since 1966 the Colorado has rearranged the rocks in Crystal Rapid several times. High water resulting from a flood of the Little Colorado River in 1972 created a second monster hole. But with Glen Canyon Dam controlling the flow, the Colorado seldom exceeded 25,000 cubic feet per second from 1966 to 1982 and was usually much lower. But then came the year of the flood: 1983. Large amounts of rain and snow, the result of a weather condition known as "El Niño," surprised the Bureau of Reclamation.

Lake Powell was almost filled to capacity when the unanticipated
record spring runoff hit. With water lapping at the top of Glen
Canyon Dam, the Bureau had no alternative but to open all the
stops including the huge diversion tunnels that bypassed the
dam. Flows through the Grand Canyon reached 48,000 cubic
feet per second on June 8, 1983, 70,000 on June 24, 92,000 on
June 27, and before the end of the month, topped out at 96,200.
At Crystal, the suddenly mighty Colorado eroded the debris left
by the 1966 flood. The start of the rapid moved upstream and
the tongue became unbelievably fast and steep. Oblique or lateral waves began on the right shore and fed the towering New
Wave at the end of the tongue. To its left and downstream, a
long wave almost parallel to the shore appeared off the mouth of
Slate Creek. The main flow continued through a hundred yards
of eight to ten foot waves to the old hole. When flows exceeded
60,000 cubic feet the hole in Crystal became truly awesome,
surging to an estimated twenty-seven feet in height and one hundred feet in width. The wave broke back upstream with the
sound of thunder. You heard the boom-boom-boom at roughly
seven-second intervals long before you saw the rapid.

From a boatman's perspective, the run of Crystal begins in-
nocently enough on a lush bed of grass on the right bank above
the rapid. Carefully, boats are tied to the trunks of tamarisk.
Some boatmen walk down along the river, but many elect to
climb the one-hundred-foot cutbank left by the Crystal Creek
flood. In the summer it always seems oven-hot among the cactus
on the trail, and the heat increases with each step away from the
river. From the top of the rise, the Colorado sweeps around Crystal's huge fan-shaped delta in a seething white arch. The tailwaves of the rapid disappear beyond a bend a half mile downstream. Crystal is, in fact, one of the Grand Canyon's longest
rapids.

From this distance a rapid cannot be read properly, so the
boatmen scramble down the steep slope to Crystal's floodplain,
where they vanish in head-high vegetation. Thrashing through it,
they come to a small, clear stream; the innocuous trickle is notorious Crystal Creek. At the edge of the Colorado the tempera-

ture drops fifteen degrees, and the ominous roar peculiar to really big rapids fills the air. River runners stand like herons on beautifully-rounded pink and orange rocks brought down by Crystal Creek from cliffs thousands of feet above. Looking up the Colorado, the tongue of Crystal Rapid appears broad and silky, but the smoothness is deceptive. The water actually powers down Crystal's initial drop at speeds approaching thirty miles per hour.

Experienced eyes immediately see a host of problems. The oblique waves to the right of the tongue can flip a boat that does not hit them straight. Or they can surf floating objects back out into the New Wave which has obvious flip potential. Surviving that, a boat can be thrown sideways against the Slate Creek Lateral and dump. And the Old Hole is still there, although not quite as steep as in the pre-1983 era. But get in it sideways and there is an excellent chance of coming out top side down. If Crystal ended with the Old Hole it would be formidable enough, but the Rock Garden is still to come. Composed of truck-sized rocks brought down in the 1966 flood, it begins with a deceptively pretty block of pink Supai Sandstone against which many boats have smashed and wrapped. Below Big Pink, the Rock Garden spreads out in a chaos of whitewater with stone fangs just beneath the waves.

Finally, way downstream and almost out of sight from the scouting point, the Colorado slows, and there on the right shore is Thank-God Eddy where upset boats and swimmers sometimes come to rest. If they don't, Tuna Creek Rapid with its 90-degree left bend and a midstream boulder sometimes called Nixon Rock (because it's hard to get "right" of it) lie in wait. A person who swims in Crystal could easily wash several miles downstream. It is hard to put this thought from your mind as you walk back to the boats for the start of the run. It's definitely nervous time; the trip leader who once proposed lunch after scouting Crystal faced a mutiny of the crew. It's time to run, not relax. The ABC (Alive Below Crystal) Party can wait for the evening.

The key to running the new Crystal in the 20,000-plus cubic feet per second flows now common is the entry—the cut off that powerful, raging tongue. It has to be made with enough momentum to crack the laterals, and it has to be precise—as close as possible to the uppermost guard rock and perpendicular to the waves surging out from the right bank. Do it perfectly (assuming the river gods are with you), and there is at least the chance of missing the New Wave altogether, catching the calm water on the right and pulling in just yards below the tongue at the feet of the admiring spectators. But the best laid plans . . .

Anyhow, start with a positive mental image. Tim Cooper, Grand Canyon Dory boatman, tells how he likes to get Crystal right in his mind before he tries it with oars. From shore he imagines the run in his mind:

> Now. Off the right shoulder of that. At the top, *there.* The stern eye 6¼ inches outside of that little wave-u-let there and going mach II, oars cocked—as the first coat of paint hits that lateral—boom—every sympathetic muscle fiber contracts and the power goes up the spine and out to the tip of the oars and the boat is fairly launched out of the water, travels a short distance through the air, and lands—plop—in the dead water just above the corner. Right.

So much for fantasy, but Cooper knows the only guarantee is that "these next will be vivid moments." And he remembers his last run in Crystal:

> We must have hit the lateral about there. Pretty close to the mark, but suddenly we're going nowhere but sideways. Pulled my face down against the "D" ring as hard as I could. Gray tubes twisting around like a strand of DNA. Front was completely upside down before the oarlocks even got to the wave. A positive, wrenching, violent flip. Then white noise and darkness.

And what is sometimes euphemistically called an adventure swim.

Sometimes nothing seems to work in Crystal. You line up carefully—standing in an effort to see the marker rocks over that impossibly-steep tongue—pull like hell at the right moment, look up and there is the New Wave right in your face. Straighten out! High side! If you get through with two oars, right is still the right direction. Maybe you'll get sufficiently out of the wave chain to clip the corner of the Old Hole and be surfed right of the Rock Garden. Maybe you can even make the lovely little beach tucked in behind the Crystal Creek delta. If not, deal with the Rock Garden as best you can. Shake and bake, shuck and jive, miss as much as you can. There is even a highway of sorts down the left side of the Garden, but it's a last resort for boats that eat too much of the Old Hole. And finally, wonderfully, there is Thank-God Eddy and the euphoric feeling of surviving a Big Drop.

In its relatively short life Crystal has produced an abundance of horror stories. There are the big pontoons that stop so suddenly in the holes that anything not tied down, like passengers, continue downstream on their own. Good, well-secured life preservers and wetsuits are special friends in such situations. In other scenarios people and equipment are painfully scrambled on the deck of a bucking pontoon. Some triple-rigs have actually folded up in Crystal. This occurs when the front boat of the three-boat lash-up rises so sharply on a wave that it folds on top of the middle boat. The resulting rubber sandwich with people and equipment in the middle is difficult to untangle. Fortunately, there is usually an air pocket between the folded boats, permitting people to breathe until the rapid ends. A variation finds the rear boat folded under the first two, which have been stopped by the steep face of a wave. The river tears loose the passengers in the underfolded boat, washing them under the entire rig and on down the river.

Dozens of boats hit the notorious pink rock at the top of the Garden every season. The lucky ones spin off it to pound down through the boulder field beyond. The less fortunate are punctured or splintered and limp downstream. And a few boats wrap around it and stay there. Wrapping is, in the estimation of many, the worst fate that can befall a riverboat. In an upset, at least, the boat washes downstream where it can usually be recovered and righted. But a wrapped boat is bent around a rock and pinned there by the force of moving water. Some boats can be freed using lines from shore, but often they remain wrapped until the river shreds them into rubber ribbons or wooden or metal splinters.

The most famous wrap on the pink rock in Crystal involved the thirty-foot inflatable pontoon of a prominent river guide. It was motor-propelled and carried about a dozen people. Out of control after wallowing through the Old Hole, the pontoon struck the pink rock sideways. The speeding Colorado immediately bent both ends downstream. The boat was securely wrapped. Floundering out of the swamped side of their boat, passengers and crew perched on the exposed upper tubes like turtles on a log while Crystal Rapid raged around them.

There was no assistance from shore, and the boatmen soon determined that they could not dislodge four thousand pounds of firmly pinned rubber. It then became necessary to tell the frightened passengers some good news and some bad news. The former concerned the water level of the Colorado: when the wrap occurred it was low, the result of curtailed nighttime water releases from the Glen Canyon Dam 112 miles upstream. The river could be expected to rise and wash the boat free. Now the bad news: high water would not occur until the next day. It would be necessary to spend the night in the middle of the rapid.

As darkness descended, the boatmen secured lines to the pink rock to prevent the boat from coming loose during the night. Then, in a commendable show of poise, they served dinner. One of the supply cans was fished from the whitewater racing through the boat, and cold food was distributed to those who had stomachs for it under the circumstances. There was little rest in "camp" that night. As expected, the Colorado began to rise about midnight. The boat might have been released from the rock, but the boatmen were afraid of a night run of the lower part of Crystal and kept the lines in place. The first light of morning found the pink rock nearly submerged, the rising river tearing at the pontoon, and its occupants cowering on the small area that was not awash. The mooring lines, normally an inch in diameter, were reduced to the thickness of a pencil under the strain. Simultaneously three persons touched knives to the taut rope, which parted with a sound like pistol shots. Then the pontoon continued on the longest run of a Big Drop ever made.

Inflatables usually bounce off rocks, but rowers of hard boats, like dories, have reasons for special fear of close encounters with Crystal's notorious Rock Garden. On one occasion a dory named the *Lava Cliff* flipped in the New Wave and piled up against a rock in the island with sprung hatches and holes in its sides. As it sank, the two boatmen aboard abandoned ship. Two days later at a lower flow the dory reappeared bent around a boulder. Anxious to recover its cargo, or at least remove debris from the river, the outfitter arranged for the National Park Service to send a helicopter to the scene. A ranger was lowered onto the wreck and attached steel cables. A winch on shore pried the boat loose, but as it swung downstream the cables snapped. The *Lava Cliff*, like its namesake rapid buried under Lake Mead, vanished for good.

Once a commercial raft trip reached Crystal in considerable disarray. One of the boatmen had flipped upstream in Granite, and the sight of the rapid at Mile 99 caused him to lose his nerve completely. Against the protestations of the trip leader, he proceeded to try to line his boat around the top of the rapid. Ropes were rigged to the bow and stern "D" rings and tied to rocks on shore, but the boat ended sawing back and forth on the face of the right-side lateral wave. It was only a matter of time before the river prevailed over the patches of neoprene on the boat. Breaking loose, the unoccupied boat wallowed into the rapid and, remarkably, survived the Old Hole and continued downstream and out of sight. Dismayed, the trip leader raced back to his raft and gave chase. He ran Crystal successfully and caught the runaway several miles below at Agate Rapid. Good work, but now twenty people were left with two boats and limited camping equipment at Crystal. Even if the customers walked around the rapid, there was no way to proceed downstream, and darkness was falling. There was no alternative but to construct a makeshift camp on the rocks and hitch a ride on motor-powered pontoons the next day. One advantage of the crowded conditions in the Grand Canyon, compared to the old days, is that in the event of trouble there is always another trip coming down the river.

The prospect of running Crystal is unnerving enough in itself, but when coupled with other causes of anxiety, it is more than most boatmen can bear. On June 15, 1986, a Grand Canyon Dory trip was just landing to scout the rapid when its members noticed a very low-flying aircraft just north of the Colorado. A moment later there was a flash and a terrific explosion. A helicopter had collided with a sightseeing plane almost directly above Crystal Creek. Twenty-five persons died in the crash. Some people actually saw the crash and the bodies raining down. Despite their feeling that low-flying aircraft had no place over designated wilderness like the inner Grand Canyon, the boatmen were badly shaken. After radioing for help, they tried to concentrate on Crystal. The first boat through caved in both its bow and stern in the Rock Garden. The remaining boatmen opted for a laborious portage over the boulders on the delta.

Crystal made river legend fast during the high water of June 1983. Many boatmen were unprepared for the new look of the rapid and the size of its exploding waves. Pontoon drivers, who normally do not scout even Big Drops, paid a high price. Several rigs flipped, and one huge inflatable actually landed on top of a companion pontoon that was recycling in the Old Hole. Passengers, many of whom were injured, had difficulty getting out of the raging river. People were strewn on both sides of the Colorado for several miles below Crystal. There was one fatality and over eighty helicopter evacuations. Crystal made headlines around the country. For a short time the National Park Service endeavored to close the river to boating but eventually opted to station a ranger at Crystal to monitor the runs.

In general, smaller oar-powered boats had less trouble at Crystal in the flood of 1983 because the swollen river permitted an extreme right-side entry. My own run with a Grand Canyon Dories trip that I was leading occurred at 72,000 cubic feet per second and was uneventful. I entered between the tops of tamarisk trees that I normally walked through to scout the rapid and pulled far right of trouble. But I saw the upside down pontoon that the outfitter allowed to float on its own out of the Grand Canyon, and I picked gear out of the river for several days. But the most exciting sight was a single, bright headlight that pierced the darkness of the river near my camp a hundred miles below Crystal. Behind it was a dory and three weary boatmen. Kenton Grua, Rudi Petschek, and Steve Reynolds were three-quarters of the way through their "speed run." The idea was to take advantage of the high water to make the fastest oar-powered traverse of the Grand Canyon. But Crystal had other ideas. After rowing all night, they reached it in mid-morning. In retrospect, they should have scouted, but a ranger on shore was screaming at them, and the legality of their trip was somewhat clouded. Unaware of the New Wave that had recently formed in Crystal, the speed runners raced down the tongue and promptly flipped. They went through the Rock Garden clinging to the dory and finally righted it in Thank-God Eddy. Pressing on, Grua, Petschek, and Reynolds passed my camp about 9 P.M. and reached the Grand Wash Cliffs and the end of the Grand Canyon exactly thirty-six hours, thirty-eight minutes and twenty seconds after launching at Lee's Ferry two hundred and seventy-nine miles upstream. Life in the fast lane!

The dam releases that changed Crystal and powered the speed runners are a reminder that the flow of the Colorado in the Grand Canyon is now artificial. The water in the river is not a result of natural processes but rather a gift from the engineers who control Glen Canyon Dam. Completed in 1963, its water release schedule is, in turn, a function of the hydroelectric power needs of metropolitan centers in the Southwest. A sweltering day (and the need for air conditioning) in Phoenix and Los Angeles means high water in the Grand Canyon. The Glen Canyon "tides" are a fact of modern river life in the canyon.

For some river runners this artificiality is disturbing. It detracts from the wilderness experience many enter the canyon to find. Although obviously not visible at Crystal Rapid, Glen Canyon Dam is a psychological factor, an unseen presence. Its importance cannot be dismissed since, in the last analysis, wilderness is a state of mind. But the full balance sheet must be read. The dam gives as well as takes away. It has, for example, created the opportunity to catch trout in the cold waters released from the bottom of Lake Powell. Trout habitat now exists all the way down to Crystal. Glen Canyon Dam also extends the river running season. In the predam days it was either feast or famine, too much water or too little. During the spring flood the old Colorado normally reached flows of 100,000 cubic feet per second and at least once in recorded history (in 1884) topped 300,000. The reason for that was the record precipitation produced by atmospheric disturbances resulting from the explosion of the volcano Krakatoa in the Java Sea—a fact of interest to proponents of the "nuclear winter" theory. But the low flows of late summer were historically less than 2,000 cubic feet per second. John Wesley Powell saw rocks today's river runners don't know exist. From April to October, they can usually count on flows in the 10,000 to 15,000 range, ideal for boating.

Occurring simultaneously with the great rain of 1966 that brought the rocks down Crystal Creek, another storm threatened to have a profound effect on Crystal and the whole Grand Canyon. This one was political, its "drainage" the halls of Congress and its subject dams. Soon after the completion of Glen Canyon Dam in 1963, federal agencies announced plans for more dams on the Colorado, and this time the Grand Canyon itself was the target. The two-thousand-foot drop of the Colorado River through its largest canyon was too much for the Bureau of Reclamation to resist. To wring the most hydroelectric power from the river, they proposed two dams. One in Marble Canyon (actually the first part of the Grand Canyon) would have created a reservoir fifty-three miles long, extending almost to the base of Glen Canyon Dam. This was the kind of total utilization of a river efficient engineers relish despite the deathblow it deals to diversity of environment and experience, not to speak of the creatures who live along rivers. A second dam in the lower reaches of Grand Canyon would have backed water up a hundred miles and claimed Lava Falls as one of its victims.

Crystal Rapid, located between the proposed upper dam and

the intended head of the lower reservoir, would have been spared. But to what fate? Along with the dams, engineers developed plans for a diversion tunnel under the Kaibab Plateau that would carry water from the upper reservoir into the Kanab Creek drainage to spin the turbines of yet another powerhouse. Since Kanab Creek is downstream from Crystal, had the tunnel been built the flow in the Colorado at Crystal would have seldom been more than a trickle. For all practical purposes river running in the Grand Canyon would have ended.

Few realize how close these projects came to being approved by Congress and the Johnson administration in 1965 and 1966. At that time the sport of running rivers was in its infancy, and few knew the Grand Canyon's rapids firsthand. Dams, on the other hand, were objects of national celebration. They made possible the growth and development that until the 1960s had been unquestioned American gods. Fortunately for the river, there were a few iconoclasts like David R. Brower and Martin Litton. Brower, the charismatic executive director of the Sierra Club, placed advertisements in nationally prominent newspapers in the summer of 1966. Litton publicized what was at stake in spectacular films and photographs. Public outrage began to build. Important, too, was the 1967 journey through the Grand Canyon of Secretary of the Interior Stewart L. Udall and his family. For two weeks Udall ran with veteran outfitter Jack Currey, and his mid-June trip was among the first to negotiate the recently remodeled Crystal Rapid. It is not hard to imagine the dryness in Currey's throat as he found a Big Drop in place of the minor rapid he was accustomed to seeing at the mouth of Crystal Creek. Having a cabinet member in the boat only added to the tension of the moment. But Currey, using an outboard motor for power, slipped through unscathed. Udall came away from his Grand Canyon experience convinced that a wild river was its own best argument for existence. "The burden of proof," Udall declared in a subsequent article, ". . . rests on the dam builders. If they cannot make out a compelling case, [Grand Canyon National Park] should be enlarged and given permanent protection." That the Grand Canyon dams were intended to make money to pay for pumping water to Phoenix was not a persuasive argument even for an Arizonan like Udall.

Under continued pressure from a citizenry who felt there were already enough dams on the Colorado, Congress gradually retreated from the brink of a pro-dam decision. In the summer of 1968 a bill authorizing the Central Arizona Project was approved without either of the Grand Canyon dams. Except for a few die-hard western congressmen and rabid developers, Americans agreed that the nation was not yet so poor that it had to fund development by damming the Grand Canyon. Conversely, it was no longer so rich that it could afford to sacrifice environmental treasures like Crystal, Lava Falls, and the free-flowing Colorado in the Grand Canyon.

No sooner had the Grand Canyon dam controversy been settled in favor of whitewater rather than kilowatts than another problem loomed over Crystal. Ironically, this one was the product of too many friends rather than too few. Rivers, it was becoming apparent, could be loved to death. From the standpoint of wilderness values too many river runners posed the same problem as too many dams. The issue centered on the concept of carrying capacity, the number of persons who could enter and enjoy a wilderness without disrupting its wilderness qualities. The impact of visitors on wildlife, beaches, and vegetation was comparatively easy to calculate. More tricky, and ultimately more crucial, was the impact of people on each other. Clearly there was a point (the psychological carrying capacity of a wilderness) at which the admission of more people ended anyone's chance of having a wilderness experience. It still might be fun in the sense that Disneyland is fun, but it would not be the kind of pleasure associated with being in wild country.

Although it is hard to believe in view of the expeditionary character of early Grand Canyon voyages, the Colorado River has actually become overcrowded. Statistics tell the story:

Travel on the Colorado River Through the Grand Canyon

Year	Number of People	Year	Number of People
1867	1?	1963-64	44
1869-1940	73	1965	547
1941	4	1966	1,067
1942	8	1967	2,099
1943	0	1968	3,609
1944	0	1969	6,019
1945	0	1970	9,935
1946	0	1971	10,385
1947	4	1972	16,432
1948	6	1973	15,219
1949	12	1974	14,253
1950	7	1975	14,305
1951	29	1976	13,912
1952	19	1977	11,830
1953	31	1978	14,356
1954	21	1979	14,678
1955	70	1980	15,142
1956	55	1981	17,038
1957	135	1982	16,949
1958	80	1983	15,443
1959	120	1984	15,952
1960	205	1985	18,113
1961	255	1986	21,168
1962	372	1987	18,008
		1988	22,088

As a consequence of the limited access points for the Grand Canyon river trip, these figures are very accurate. The possible single passage in 1867 was that of James White (see pages 185-187). In 1963-1964 the closing of the gates of Glen Canyon Dam so Lake Powell could fill precluded running the Grand Canyon for all but forty-four individuals willing to drag their boats from pool to pool. After the 1972 season the National Park Service began to limit the number of persons permitted to make the run to that year's level, and unforeseen cancellations kept use below the limit in the succeeding years. A drought in 1977 compelled the Bureau of Reclamation to cut releases from Glen Canyon Dam drastically and thereby eliminate several months of river travel through the Grand Canyon.

Current management policy, allegedly based on extensive research into visitor impact, controls river use through the allocation of "user-days" (one person on the river for one day is one user-day). At present, the river management plan allows for a maximum annual use of 169,950 user-days. The actual volume of people in the canyon tends to stay fairly constant under this plan; the number of *individuals* taking trips may vary from year to year. The apparent increase in use from 1987 to 1988, for example, may reflect changing policies of some commercial outfitters. A commercial company can sell three segmented trips (Lee's Ferry to Phantom Ranch, Phantom to Whitmore Wash, and Whitmore to Lake Mead) to three individuals, or one full trip to one person. The user-days (and presumably, canyon impact) are the same, but total river use appears to increase in the first case. Nevertheless, there are abuses of this system. The excessive use in 1986 resulted from commercial outfitters overbooking their trips, and the 21,168 does not even reflect commercial crews and national park ranger patrols.

The number of people who want to run the river, particularly those who want noncommercial or private trips rises every year, and the allocation ratio for commercial and private trips has been a controversial issue. Currently, the National Park Service limits the do-it-yourselfers to one-third of the total user-day allotment. There are now about 4,000 names on the waiting list for a private permit, representing a six-year wait. The resulting competition for noncommercial permits is one of the unhappy consequences of the growing popularity of whitewater boating.

The big story in these statistics is the astonishing growth of river running after 1965. This is, of course, related to the increased interest on the part of many Americans in temporary alternatives to their largely urbanized way of life. Far from being the adversary it was to pioneers, wilderness is a refreshing novelty to the modern American, whose normal existence might be characterized as overcivilized. Solitude, challenge, danger, self-sufficiency, and humility in the face of natural forces are increasingly rare and increasingly coveted. The search for them brings people to Big Drops.

Another factor that changed river running from a daredevil stunt to a family sport is the equipment revolution. Just as back-packing benefitted from the advent of lightweight pack frames, food, stoves, and tents, the river runner's world changed radically with the availability after World War II of inflatable rubber boats. Capable of bouncing off rather than smashing on rocks, the inflatables are also unsinkable, maneuverable, and comfortable. They are the reason why a rapid like Crystal is run rather than lined or portaged as it surely would have been by the early runners (and was, on occasion, by early wooden boat operators like Gaylord Staveley and Martin Litton). The new boats are magic carpets that take people easily, perhaps too easily in view of the numbers, into the wilderness.

In the case of the Grand Canyon, the publicity surrounding the dam controversy also proved a direct stimulant to river travel. Films, books, and articles allowed millions to discover what the canyon had to offer. In the space of a few years after the struggle against the dams began in the mid-1960s, the Grand Canyon river trip became the classic American wilderness experience. Responding to and in some ways accelerating this demand, commercial river outfitters sprouted overnight. By 1971 twenty-one companies had obtained licenses to conduct trips in the Grand Canyon. Even at costs that reach $1800 per person, the commercial quota (86.5 percent of total use) is always fully utilized. People seem to understand that there are a few things lovers of wilderness adventure just *have* to do—and running the Colorado River through the Grand Canyon is one of them.

Amid all the issues surrounding its management, the Colorado still runs free through Crystal Rapid. At the present level of visitation it is common on the typical summer day to find another party or two inspecting or running the rapid. Watching other boats may lessen the sense of pioneering, but it does nothing to diminish the need of each boatman to execute his task perfectly. The wilderness setting is, of course, important, but were a Big Drop located on the Hudson River adjacent to New York City, it would still be a Big Drop. The challenge of controlling a boat on fast water remains. No matter how many times you have boated the Grand, things get very serious at Mile 98.25. Crystal can devour the best boatmen on the river; nothing is guaranteed when you start down that curving tongue. River runners sometimes hate Crystal, but it keeps the Grand Canyon river experience honest. Most everywhere else it's mostly fun and games. But as Tim Cooper puts it, "Crystal is different. The grizzly bear of the Grand Canyon. What do you do with it? Occasionally eats a tourist. Shoot the Bastard? Wouldn't be the same place without it."

Indeed!

You're safer riding a boat . . . through the Grand Canyon . . . than you are driving your car to work every day for a year. That is what the statistics seem to mean. But despite the odds, despite the proven efficacy of a sound life jacket, there is still something about a big rapid that makes a man nervous. Every time.

EDWARD ABBEY

Lava Falls

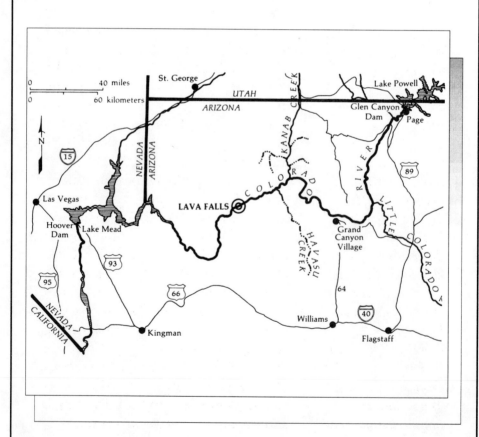

Chapter 10

Once on the tongue, I faced downstream and braced myself, as my boat gathered speed with every yard. Then with a great hiss the first wave was upon us. The boat reared skyward, perched on top for an instant like the cap on a mushroom, then plunged into the trough beyond. Up, down, up, down, we hurtled. Jets of spray stung our faces; the roar of the rapid drowned out our voices. I strained at the oars to keep the boat headed into the waves and avert a broach which could lead to an upset. Gradually, I pulled to the right, out of the main current; and at last, my lungs heaving from

You never really finish running Lava Falls. Asked on the river the night before Lava if he was ready for the rapid, a Grand Canyon boatman said he hoped so because he had run it four hundred times that winter—driving to work every morning and before sleeping each night. Few rapids in the world grip the mind that way; few have the ability to condense a year, a lifetime on moving water into forty-five pounding seconds. Lava does. It is an undisputed Big Drop. Season after season, high water and low, kayaks to pontoons, Lava has a strong claim to being the most difficult stretch of runnable whitewater in the West. Sure, the new, post-1983 Crystal may scare boatmen more, especially at high water, but there is a way to cheat Crystal. A perfect run pops over six-foot lateral waves and slides into calm water far right of the monster waves and holes. Five seconds and it's over. There is no way to cheat Lava Falls. Right entry, the slot or left side, you end up in the soup, the deep yogurt, fighting chaotic fifteen-foot waves as if your life depended upon it—which it just may.

The climax of every trip in the Grand Canyon is Lava Falls. The length and rhythm of the Grand Canyon river *the effort and my arm muscles knotting with cramps, I reached the eddy and rowed triumphantly to the beach. Between hitting the tongue and hitting the beach, perhaps a minute had elapsed.*

FRANCOIS LEYDET

trip reinforce this perception. From the put-in at Lee's Ferry, Arizona, the trip is either 188 miles to Whitmore Wash, 225 miles to the take-out at Diamond Creek, or 279 miles to Lake Mead. The Colorado crashes through Lava Falls at mile 179.2, near the end of any trip. It is the last major rapid, a final showdown with the river. There is big stuff upstream, of course, and for a time the business of running it obscures what is waiting just below mile 179. But Lava has a way of creeping into the consciousness and conversation of people on the river. "You think that's big?" a boatman will shout over the screams of passengers in the tailwaves of a rapid in the upper canyon, "Wait until we get to Lava!" Or he thinks to himself after a sloppy run, "I better not do that in Lava." Someone quietly puts aside a cigar or a can of beer for "after Lava." So the reputation grows, and even those who are new to the Colorado quickly sense that Lava Falls is something special. "How big is this rapid compared to Lava?" they invariably ask. Or, "When do we get to Lava?" Or, more to the point, "Can you walk around Lava?"

Sometimes humor covers the anxiety. "I'll bet you can't keep that cigar lit through Lava," someone challenges. Once a group finds out that you can walk around the falls, there are endless jokes about chickening out. But behind the comic facade every river runner begins to sense the necessity of a personal confrontation with the big one. And he wonders, secretly, if he *will* want to walk around.

Occasionally a person new to the Grand Canyon will get fed up with the steady diet of Lava talk. Lava Falls cannot be much tougher than what they have seen in the many miles from Lee's Ferry; it is just the boatmen's way of keeping up interest until the end of a long trip. But things look different on the downstream side. As one upstream doubter who had just been through Lava Falls exclaimed, "That rapid should be called 'Evangelist,' it made a *believer* out of me!"

So it is that a Grand Canyon river trip unfolds with Lava Falls looming over the minds of river runners as the Redwall lime-stone looms over the river itself. Tension builds once Crystal, be-low Mile 98, has been passed. The next few days are not so tough, and there is time to think ahead. Some groups plan Lava parties and relish what they will eat and drink and smoke after getting through. Some compose songs about the rapid. Others write poetry. Jack Reynolds's "The Hole" commemorates the time "late in May/when I approached Lava Falls in the heat of the day." The water, we learn, was very low, but from the end of the rapid issued an "unusual roar." When Jack went to look:

My jaw dropped down in disbelief
For there it was in awesome relief,
A monstrous hole ten feet wide
And one mile deep!

Others take the familiar Christmas fable and turn it into:

'Twas the night before Lava
And all through the camp
The boatmen were pacing
Their armpits were damp.
Their life vests were hung
On their bow lines with care
In hope that the river gods
Would answer their prayers.

In truth, though, most boatmen try to appear nonchalant above the rapid. Occasionally you catch them staring into space. In their minds they are rehearsing, like a springboard diver, the moves and decisions they will have to make at Lava Falls.

It is hard to think of much else than the rapid the night before Lava. After an afternoon playing in blue-green Havasu Creek, most parties camp near National Canyon, mile 166, just as John Wesley Powell did on August 24, 1869. This leaves twelve miles to Lava Falls. They are slow miles; in places there is little surface current to move the boats downstream. Motorpowered rigs blast through the lakes above Lava. Oarsmen slog it out, stroke after stroke.

There never seems a great deal to say on Lava Day. The boatmen turn inward, absorbed in their own thoughts, tinkering with knots and equipment. They know that a Grand Canyon trip with oars requires about seventy hours of time on the river. Almost anyone can handle a boat safely except for ten minutes of this time. But in those ten minutes—minutes spent positioning above or maneuvering in the biggest rapids—boatmen earn their pay. There are only a few tongues or slots you have to hit in the Grand Canyon, but, in the carefully measured words of veteran outfitter Ron Smith, "You better hit them!" Lava Falls is one such moment, one such place. The boatmen, who at other times might be tour guides, cooks, comedians, lovers, and naturalists, become simply rowers of boats. It is time to concentrate on basics. The passengers seem to understand this. After a week on the water they tend to take the boatmen for granted, but Lava creates new respect born of new anxiety.

At Cove Canyon, five miles above Lava Falls, the Colorado makes a gradual swing to the west and slows still more. Here the inner canyon walls are three thousand feet high. From the Toroweap Overlook it is possible to toss a stone directly into the river. One of the world's most dramatic displays of volcanic activity begins here. About one million years ago, long after the Grand Canyon had been cut nearly to its present depth, eruptions of molten rock along the structurally weak Toroweap fault caused radical topographic transformations. Lava poured from a

number of vents, chiefly to the north of the Colorado, and covered thousands of acres, some of it flowing down to the river.
Looking at the lava cascades, long since cooled into basalt rock,
that blacken the cliffs like thick paint, John Wesley Powell wrote
in 1869: "What a conflict of water and fire there must have been
here! Just imagine a river of molten rock running down into a
river of melted snow. What a seething and boiling of the waters;
what clouds of steam rolled into the heavens!"

One result of this awesome geologic spectacle was a dam—
really a series of them corresponding to the several lava flows—
that effectively plugged the Colorado River. Estimates of the
height of the lava dams vary from six-hundred to fifteen-hun-
dred feet. A block of the larger size would have created a lake in
the Grand Canyon extending all the 179 miles back to Lee's
Ferry. After the initial flows, the new lake gradually filled, and in
view of the volume of water carried by the prehistoric Colorado
it probably did not require many years. There then commenced
one of earth history's great confrontations of rock and moving
water. When the rising lake reached the top of the natural dam,
it began to pour over and to wear away the dam. As the impedi-
ment broke down for thousands of years, the Colorado must
have raged through seventy miles of lava debris in a Big Drop to
end comparison. Basalt is extremely hard, but time always favors
the river. Little by little the Colorado scoured its lava-blocked
channel in the same way it had cut through a mile of rock to
form the Grand Canyon. By the time the first man peered over
the rim, perhaps five thousand years ago, the million-year battle
was almost over. All that remained was Lava Falls.

Thinking about the prehistoric lava dam at mile 179 always
brings to mind man's efforts to control the river with lesser dams
of concrete and steel. Several were proposed in the sixties for
this section of the Grand Canyon. One, Bridge Canyon, at mile
237, would have transformed ninety-three miles of river into a
flatwater impoundment. Had it been built, Lava Falls would have
become a jumble of rocks on the bottom of a lake.

In terms of longevity, manmade dams have one advantage
over natural ones: spillways. Engineers plan for water to go

through, rather than over, dams and turn turbines in the process. But the axiom still holds: the river always wins. Especially in a watershed of high siltation such as the Colorado, the dams eventually fill up with the powdered rock remains of continental erosion. No one has figured out how to keep the silt from filling the reservoir, building toward the top of the dam, and choking the spillways. Finally, as the basin silts in, a wave slightly larger than the rest washes over the lip. It is the beginning of the end for a dam, the start of the same process that wore down the old lava plug. Big dams like Hoover and Glen Canyon look eternal but they are doomed. In the long run of geologic time the river will triumph. These monuments to man's drive to control nature will be a tangle of concrete and metal debris through which the liberated river roars. And then, to use Edward Abbey's vision, our far-removed descendants will come to the edge of the canyons to look over and wonder at the origins of tremendous rapids. Of course *their* distant descendants will not see more than a scoured canyon and placid river. The debris will be mud on the floor of an ocean. The river always wins.

Vulcan's Forge—some call it his Anvil—rises directly out of the Colorado about a mile above Lava Falls. A pinnacle about a hundred feet high, it is all that remains of the central core, or neck, of an ancient volcano. The lava broke to the earth's surface directly beneath the river. The clouds of steam Powell imagined must have been enormous. Now the river grinds away at the black basalt of Vulcan's Forge, its erosive action aided by the roots of a few cactus that have managed to find a liveable niche among the lumps of solidified lava. Some river runners toss coins at the steep-sided plug of lava; if they stick, chances for a good run in Lava are thought to increase. If the coins drop into the Colorado, people may shortly do the same. So toss the coins until one sticks, take no chances, appease all gods on Lava Day. On the north rim, to the right, towers Vulcan's Throne. A mile-wide cinder cone, it was the source of much of the lava that created Lava Falls.

As Vulcan's Throne disappears behind the towering north rim of the inner gorge, the river slows still more. Big rapids exert a damming effect on moving water, pooling it for as much as a mile upstream and the Colorado takes on a lake-like quality above Lava. You try to sit, relaxed, at the oars, but it's a nervous time. Few boatmen do not eventually turn and row methodically to the right (north) bank above the rapid.

There is a little welcome shade under the tamarisk, and the boatmen tie their bow lines to the trunks of these small trees. The path to the viewpoint winds up through the lava rubble and across talus slopes to a level spot several hundred feet above the river. It is always hot here, the black basalt radiating the absorbed heat of the desert sun. You hear the rapid before you see it. The deepest and most ominous of the river's many voices surges up to tear at your confidence. No one says very much at first.

From the viewpoint almost directly over the top of Lava Falls you can see the black boulders littering the right bank. Similar rocks and ledges under water are the main cause of the astonishing behavior of the river here. But there is another factor at work in creating Lava. From the south a major canyon, Prospect, cut along the Toroweap fault line, joins the Grand. In its times of flood, Prospect Canyon has pushed a gravel fan into the Colorado and scattered the quarter-mile of boulders that cause problems on the left side of the rapid.

At Lava Falls the Colorado drops thirty-seven vertical feet; twenty feet of this occurs in an astonishing hundred yards at the top of the rapid—a rate of descent that Robert B. Stanton, with his engineer's eye, extrapolated at 352 feet per mile on his 1890 Colorado River survey. From above you watch the smooth, slick water gather speed as it approaches the lip. In a boat, floating toward the main falls, all you see is a line across the river and, far beyond, the tops of tailwaves.

From the scouting point above the rapid you look at the tongue of smooth water funneling at an impossibly steep angle down the right side of the falls toward two sets of enormous "V" waves. A hundred yards of irregular ten-foot waves follows. Then comes the biggest standing wave most boatmen will ever see. Among printable descriptions, it is most commonly called "the Big Wave in Lava." The hole-wave complex occurs where the strong flow from the left of the falls meets the right-hand current caroming off an enormous lava block jutting from the right bank. Periodically, in a cycle of five to seven seconds, this wave "explodes." The energy of the moving water within it becomes so great that the wave breaks backwards on itself in a fury of white-water. On the United States Geological Survey's 1923 trip, boat-man Lewis R. Freeman reported that at a flow of 125,000 cubic feet per second this upstream breaking wave compressed air which jetted out from its sides in the manner of a blowhole in the rocks on an ocean shore. These unusual conditions were the result of unseasonal rains that raised the river level twenty-one feet in twenty-four hours.

In 1957 P.T. Reilly encountered a flow of about the same magnitude. The Big Wave was cycling at about twelve-second in-tervals, and it covered nearly half the swollen river. The periodic explosion sent spray flying over both banks of a river a hundred yards wide! Curiously, between the explosions, there are intervals when the huge wave is relatively smooth and regular in shape. It is a question of timing, an element over which the river runner has no control. If the wave explodes in your face, too bad. The next boat could sail right over. The river gods have the last word.

After the big one, Lava's tailwaves taper off to fifteen feet, twelve feet, eight feet. But that is at a flow of less than 30,000 cu-bic feet per second, the normal maximum since the placement of Glen Canyon Dam upstream. It was different during the great runoffs of the predam era such as the estimated 300,000 cubic feet per second flow of 1884. Huge coffee-colored tailwaves must have continued right down to the cliff on the left a quarter-mile below the end of the modern rapid. Indeed, the possibility of be-ing pounded against the cliff in Lower Lava would have been the most terrifying part of running a high-flow Lava Falls before the upstream dam. Across the river, just upstream of the cliff, there is a flash as hot springs gush through a thicket of head-high saw-grass and plunge over the bank into the Colorado. Their pres-ence is a reminder that the earth fires which created this place still burn deep under the Toroweap fault.

After a time alone the boatmen ritually gather on a large flat-topped hunk of lava directly above the start of the rapid. "Where're ya' goin'?" someone grunts, and the group begins to compare possible routes, pointing and gesturing in an effort to identify waves that in the surprising scale of the Grand Canyon are still a quarter-mile away.

Study of the rapid reveals several possible runs. At flows above 20,000 cubic feet per second, most boatmen prefer a run left of the main or ledge falls. It begins very close to the left bank, follows a line of broken water at the edge of the tongue and involves a power-pull over lateral waves and down a steep wall of water into the jumbled waves below the falls. At this point nothing is certain. You can be hammered, filled, deprived of one or two oars, turned stern first or flipped. Or you can slide through as though the Red Sea parted without taking on more than a bucket or two. It all depends on the hydraulics of the moment. Memorable left runs miss the Big Wave and most of the tailwaves completely. But you can run left, be surfed right, and find the big fellow right in your face.

The second option in Lava is the so-called "slot run." It is generally attractive (relatively speaking) at flows below 20,000 but more than 12,000 cubic feet per second. Oracle Rock up at the National Canyon camp tells the story. Boatmen examine it on the morning of Lava Day. It if is not exposed too much there will be enough water to run the slot. The set-up for this right-side run is along an innocuous bubble line that appears on smooth water well above the rapid. Face right (ready to pull back against the strong right current), put your oarlocks over the bubbles and inch toward the white roar out of sight below. At the last second you see it: a thread of smooth water snaking between the "V" wave on the right and the main falls. Push into it and hold on for a neck-snapping jolt. Usually boats will dive down and then ride up over the backwash, but an error in entry of just a few feet can result in a spectacular bow-over-stern flip. The Maytag Treatment and a nasty swim follow immediately.

The major problem with the slot run is that you do not make it from a 200-foot-high vantage on the shore where it is clearly visible. At river level, even standing on the seat of a boat, all the boatman can see is space and an occasional blast of spray. Until the last few yards there is no way to know if the boat is heading for the slot, the falls, or the side of the "V" wave. And by that time the boat is committed. "Cues" become crucial. You try to remember how far to place your boat from this shoreline rock or that recurring swirl in the current, aiming always for something you cannot see.

On one occasion a boatman missed the slot and dropped straight over the left side of the main falls. From below, the boat appeared to hang in midair, upside down, raining people into the river. Thirty seconds later a girl hurtled over the top of the Big Wave. Her long blond pigtails, tied with bright blue ribbons, streamed straight out behind her. But when we fished her out of the river, she was smiling. Getting through Lava alive does that to people.

Then there was the dory Don Briggs captured on film that missed the left run and dropped directly over the main falls. It almost rode out over the reversing wave below, but the river said "not yet." Sucked back in, the dory turned over four times but came out right side up! By this time, of course, the people were far downstream.

The Grand Canyon Dory boatmen who ran a replica of John Wesley Powell's boat over Lava in connection with the making of the popular IMAX film also had a close encounter with the main falls—but on purpose. Although the Powell boat seemed unstable, its rowers were veterans of hundreds of Grand Canyon trips. They kept it upright through all the upstream rapids including many that Powell portaged. By the time the trip reached Lava the director of the film was desperate. He needed footage of a flip for the show, and he came to the boatmen with a proposition. For an extra $500 would they take their boat directly over the main fall? It was not an easy choice. Most of the boatmen had swum before in Lava, and they did not relish the prospect of doing it voluntarily. Still the money was on the table, and just maybe they could survive the center ledge. But as the film shows, it wasn't even a contest. The director got his footage of a flip, and the boatmen got the Maytag treatment along with their checks. Later a professional stunt man, who viewed the film, said he would not have made a deal for less than $7,000.

But this time let's make a right-side run. It is mandatory at lower flows and sometimes appeals to crazies who want the biggest ride in Lava. You walk back across the lava and down through the shoreline brush to the boats. Little things suddenly become big. You tie the laces of your tennis shoes and tie them again. You tug for the twentieth time at the belt of your life preserver, check the lines securing gear on the boat, reseat the oars in their locks. It is no time for banter. Most boatmen ask their passengers not to talk as they float back into the current. It is agonizingly slow on the way toward the lip of Lava Falls. Only in the final few yards does the river gather speed. It also veers sharply to the right, directly into a series of gaping holes. Experienced boatmen have prepared for this, positioning themselves much farther left than appears safe. A perfect entry, in fact, seems to the unknowing to be carrying a boat straight over the main falls. The last few seconds make the difference.

A properly positioned boat rises and falls over a set of smooth, but surprisingly large entrance waves. It is a delicious fluid moment of calm before the storm. Rising over these first satin waves, the whole rapid is finally visible, the huge black rock near the end seeming very far away. Immediately in front is the steep tongue. Now everything happens fast. The first "V" waves lie at the downstream end of the tongue. Some boatmen think they can "crash" the left side of this wave, but the attempt usually ends in a sideways position and a flip. The better course is to plow into the very point of the "V". Being light (you should not have shipped much water to this point), most boats will rise quickly on the side of the wave and push through it. But in the process they take on hundreds of pounds of Colorado River. That makes positioning for the second, larger "V" wave more difficult.

The lower "V" packs one of the hardest hits in whitewater boating. It has flipped every kind of boat from kayak to thirty-foot pontoon. But sometimes the wave simply stands a boat on its side and strips it of its occupants. It is also possible, of course, to

punch through in relative control of an upright boat. The next
hundred yards are a confused jumble of irregular waves. You
slant the bow left, right, left in an effort to meet them head on.
Water continues to cascade over the sides, filling boats to the
gunwales. It is important to understand that you don't get
splashed in Lava Falls; you get inundated. Eating a solid wall of
water is one of the quintessential experiences of running this
rapid. Not a few river runners have distinctly recalled being in
the boat but completely underwater and unable, for several
tense seconds, to breathe. In one astonishing run a boat flipped
over on one wave and back, right side up, on another. It required two reports of witnesses on shore to convince its confused
occupants, who never left their seats, that they went completely
around.

As you pound down the middle section of Lava Falls, you become increasingly aware of the black lava block, big as a house,
on the right shore. Awareness turns to terror as the view from
the tops of the waves make it appear that the current you are riding is pounding directly against it. Boatmen know, however, that
it would be hard to hit the rock if they wanted to. A "buffer wave"
rolling off its upstream side will carry boats around. If you have
sufficient courage and control to point your boat squarely at the
big rock, it is sometimes possible to slide between it and the giant wave immediately to its left. The price paid for trying this is
the possibility of rolling not to the left of the rock but to its right
and into a deep, angry whirlpool surrounded on three sides by
jagged rock. A wooden dory went into this potato peeler once
and came out splinters. The boatman, luckily, gained the left
buffer and escaped downstream in one piece. An aluminum
boat trapped here had to be helicoptered out and ended its career along with thousands of beer cans in a recycling plant in Las
Vegas.

Most boatmen choose not to play tag with the black rock and
instead line up as best they can for one of the biggest waves in
the Grand Canyon. When you see it from the crest of the wave
immediately upstream, it seems absolutely inconceivable that a
boat could climb anything so high and so steep. Grand Canyon

veterans learn to "push" on their oars in this situation, adding a little more momentum to the twenty miles per hour provided by the current. Combined with the weight of a nearly swamped boat, the force is sometimes enough to drive boats through the top of the wall of water. It is also possible, especially if the wave decides to "explode" in your face, to remain in the hole, caught in a dynamic balance of forces generated by the downstream current and the backward-breaking wave. Boatmen have reported starting up the wave again and again only to slide back down it into the hole. Sometimes this frightening minuet ends with the boats being squirted out the side of the hole. More often they finally catch an upstream edge, roll, and wash through. The big wave's explosion cycle is the key. You cannot time a run to catch the unpredictable moment when the hole "fills in," offering a relatively easy passage. You take your chances, and you say your prayers.

No one will ever know for certain who was the first to run Lava Falls. Perhaps it was James White. White did not really take a boat down Lava; he floated through on huge logs. The year was 1867, two years before John Wesley Powell's first expedition. White's story is astonishing. It is based entirely on the oral reports of this unlettered and unassuming frontiersman, a fact which has made it easy for subsequent river runners to dismiss the whole affair or, as the fine historian David Lavender does in his *River Runners of the Grand Canyon*, treat it as a myth or legend. But if we take James White's word for where he started and ended his 1867 trip, it is hard to deny that he did indeed pass through the Grand Canyon and over Lava Falls.

White's ordeal began in the spring of 1867 when he left Colorado City, Colorado, on a prospecting venture with two other men. Somewhere in the San Juan River drainage, considerably north of the Grand Canyon, Indians attacked the party, and one of White's companions was killed. The remaining two fled down a dry streambed to the Colorado River, where they constructed a makeshift log raft. White later remembered that they floated four days on a big calm river through yellow rock—a perfect description of Glen Canyon. After drifting past the future site of

Lee's Ferry, the character of the river changed. White recalled rapids repeatedly breaking his raft apart and finally claiming the life of White's remaining friend. By this time he was well into Marble Canyon, and there seemed no alternative but to continue riding the river. He tied himself to logs, gnawed two rawhide knife scabbards for food, and went on floating twelve to fourteen hours a day. At night he tied his raft to the shore and slept. Finally on the fourteenth day of his ordeal, September 7, 1867, he was pulled half-dead from the river by Mormon settlers at Callville, Nevada, sixty miles downstream from the Grand Wash Cliffs, which mark the end of the Grand Canyon.

In his recollections of the trip White recalled one rapid bigger than all the rest. It could have been Lava Falls. And he almost certainly floated through it. White, after all, was not scouting rapids in an effort to bring boats and equipment through the canyon. He was just trying to get out as fast as he could to save his life. If he lost one log in a rapid, he found another. There was no reason to line or portage.

White's detractors maintain he simply could not have done what he claimed, the journey was impossible, and White was a liar. But such opinions were voiced by the pioneers of Grand Canyon river running, who tended to exaggerate the difficulty of the journey to accentuate their own achievement. Reconsidered in the light of present experiences on the Colorado, White's feat seems much more plausible. What he claimed to have done is clearly possible. Men have deliberately swum the entire length of the Grand Canyon. Empty boats have floated along for miles, sometimes upside down. Driftwood regularly floats through the canyon; so could a man holding on to it. The speed of the descent of a log, allowing for time caught in eddies, would have been just about what White remembered having taken—two weeks from Glen Canyon to Callville. It would have been inconceivable to have taken that amount of time floating the sixty miles from the Grand Wash Cliffs to Callville which some feel he did instead of the Grand Canyon. White could and would have walked that far over the open desert bordering the river in two or three days. Besides, his ordeal began in western Colorado, not

northwestern Arizona. So the controversy returns again to
White's memory and his honesty. If he in fact spent so long a
time floating the Colorado as he claimed (and his physical condition when rescued suggested he did), then he must have
passed through the Grand Canyon. Moreover, 1867 was a year in
which the Colorado carried exceptionally high water. Many of
the rocks that might have killed White were covered while the
current pushed along his logs at top speed.

Still, it is pointless to celebrate James White as the first man
to "run" the Grand Canyon. John Wesley Powell's reputation is
well deserved. His was a planned achievement. White's journey
was just blind luck but remains to tantalize the imagination.
Think of a weakened, dazed man, looking up from his logs at
the line across the river, listening to the boom of Lava, and thinking, in his desperate condition, that he might as well hang on
and hope for the best. Then the sickening first drop and the
brown water tearing at his body and smashing it against the
wood and, finally, the calm below and the wondering how much
more could he take before death. He took enough to get out
barely alive and tell a tale nobody would, at first, believe.

John Wesley Powell did not run Lava on his 1869 exploratory
descent of the Colorado. His journal is quite clear. After camping the night of August 24 near National Canyon, the nine men
and three boats floated the twelve miles to Lava Falls. They
noted the evidence of volcanic activity and imagined the lava
dam that had temporarily blocked the river. Landing on the less
precipitous left bank, Powell made his decision after a quick
glance at the rapid. "We have to make a portage here," he wrote
in his journal, "which is completed in about three hours; then
on we go." And go they did. The last entry for August 25 reads:
"Thirty-five miles today. Hurrah!" Subtracting the three hours
spent portaging Lava, it was a remarkable day.

Although the Powell party bypassed Lava Falls, they made an
unexpected run three days later of a rapid that may well have
been a greater challenge. Lava Cliff Rapid, as Powell named it,
had the same physical characteristics as Lava Falls, but it is now
drowned under Lake Mead. The lava was on the north side in a

cliff a hundred feet high with huge rocks at its base. The tributary canyon, Spencer, came in from the left side as at Lava Falls,
but for some reason Powell crossed back to the right thinking he
could lower the boats from a 100-foot line off the top of the cliff.
This meant confronting the main fall of the rapid. It was a difficult moment. That very morning, six miles upstream at Separation Canyon, Powell and five followers had left three men who
had determined to desert the expedition and climb out of the
canyon. Now, above Lava Cliff, it appeared that the deserters'
doubts about getting out alive by the river route were well
founded.

Persisting with the right-side lining, Powell put one of his
best boatmen, Civil War veteran George Bradley, in the first boat
to fend off from the cliff. The others started to lower him down
the rapid. Meanwhile Powell went ahead to check on the downstream end of the cliff. To his horror he found a waterfall. Rushing back to order the men to stop, he found them already committed. The boat had been lowered to where it could not be
retrieved against the current. To make matters worse, the rope
Powell had thought would reach to the top of the cliff was too
short. Now the boat, held stationary in the current by the rope,
began to veer in and out. Each inward lurch smashed it against
the cliff despite the efforts of the desperate boatman to hold off
with an oar. It was time for quick decisions. Bradley, feeling it
better to risk the rapid than be splintered by the cliff, moved to
cut the tethering line with his knife. Just at that moment the
whole fixture to which the line was tied broke away. Powell describes the consequences:

> With perfect composure Bradley seizes the great scull oar,
> places it in the stern rowlock, and pulls with all his power (and
> he is an athlete) to turn the bow of the boat downstream . . .
> rather than to drift broadside on. One, two, strokes he makes,
> and a third just as she goes over [the main falls] and the boat is
> fairly turned, and she goes down almost beyond our sight . . .
> Then she comes up again on a great wave, and down and up,
> then around behind some great rocks, and is lost in the mad,

white foam below. We stand frozen with fear, for we see no boat. Bradley is gone! So it seems. But now, away below, we see something coming out of the waves. It is evidently a boat. A moment more and we see Bradley standing on deck, swinging his hat to show that he is all right.

Returning to his second boat, Powell and two boatmen prepared to run. Their course was almost certainly farther left than Bradley's who, after all, had been directly against the cliff when he tore loose from his line. At any rate, the first wave at the base of Lava Cliff's fall swamped Powell's boat and the second rolled it over. The men tumbled through the tailwaves, and Powell's next recollection was being lifted from a whirlpool by Bradley. But their agony was almost over; the next day, August 29, 1869, the boats floated past the Grand Wash Cliffs and out of what they called "our granite prison." The three deserters were never seen again.

Powell's second Colorado River expedition ended at Kanab Creek in September 1872, and he did not see either Lava Falls or Lava Cliff Rapid. The next river runner to pass that way was Robert B. Stanton, the engineer who dreamed of constructing a railroad along the Colorado through the Grand Canyon. He portaged Lava Falls in late February 1890. This suggests that the first men to run Lava in boats were George F. Flavell and Ramon Montéz, a Mexican he persuaded to join him for a run down the Colorado. These trappers started without fanfare at Green River, Wyoming, on August 27, 1896. Flavell was an excellent craftsman who rebuilt his skiff, the *Panthon*, twice on the upper river in anticipation of the rapids in Grand Canyon. Using the Galloway method, he ran the fifteen-foot wooden boat stern first, facing down river and pushing with his oars. Trapping beaver and taking their time, they reached the Little Colorado on October 20. Then, anxious to end the trip, Flavell blasted through to the Grand Wash Cliffs, arriving just eleven days later. They were able to accomplish this stunning feat by running the rapids rather than lining or portaging them. Flavell reported their philosophy: "If we had lowered over all the bad places, it would have taken a month." He fully expected to turn over and hit rocks in his flat-bottomed boat but he was confident about getting through. "There is only one stone we must not hit," Flavell noted, ". . . our Tomb Stone!" Unlike Powell and Stanton, Flavell was an unschooled trapper. His diary is vague and does not mention Lava Falls. But Flavell did say he ran every rapid in the Grand Canyon except Soap Creek, and his quick passage lends credence to the claim. Quite possibly George Flavell pushed the *Panthon* over the big waves below the basalt cliffs. No one witnessed the run, and no one will ever know for sure.

Although early trips down the Grand Canyon were usually years apart, Nathaniel Galloway and William Richmond were on the river just a month behind Flavell and Montéz. On this run, and on Galloway's second in 1909 guiding Julius Stone, he portaged and lined the biggest rapids including Lava Falls. In fact after meeting George Flavell on the lower Colorado in February 1897, Galloway expressed doubts that Flavell had tackled the Big Drop at mile 179.

Ellsworth and Emery Kolb ran the Grand in the winter of 1911-1912 and found Lava Falls "so filled with jagged pieces of black rock that a portage was advisable." They completed it in near-freezing conditions made tolerable only by periodic soaks in the hot pools below the rapid. The United States Geological Survey trip of 1923 also took the dry route through Lava, walking around on the left bank. Clyde Eddy and his crew of inexperienced college boys followed suit. Their account of a 1927 trip simply stated that "Lava Falls Rapid cannot possibly be run." And when the alternative is portaging a twelve-hundred-pound boat, one does not come to such a conclusion without much reflection.

If not George Flavell in 1896, then Haldane "Buzz" Holmstrom was the first person to run Lava Falls in a boat as opposed to James White's log. The short, blue-eyed Swede from Oregon had the arms of a weightlifter and a passion for wild rivers. In 1937 he ran a homemade fifteen-foot wooden boat from Green River, Utah, through the Grand Canyon, and he did it *alone*. Lava Falls was one of five rapids he portaged in eight hundred river miles. Holmstrom's journal referred to "vicious waters twisting between great blocks of lava." The next year found Buzz back on the Colorado with Amos Burg and his inflatable raft, the *Charlie.* Holmstrom's boat was again wooden and called the *Julius F* after Julius F. Stone who, although eighty-three, had sent the chronically-impoverished Buzz a check after the solo run. In 1938 Holmstrom and his companions came to Lava in late October. One member of the group wrote in his journal while Holmstrom scouted the rapid: "We believe Buzz is the best boatman in the world, but I don't suppose he will attempt to run this death trap." Wrong! Buzz knew Big Drops were the ultimate challenge of river running, and he prepared to go for it. Burg's camera documented the successful run of the *Julius F* down the right side in the low water of autumn.

With Lava Cliff and Separation Rapids almost swallowed by a rising Lake Mead and Crystal not yet transformed into a Big Drop, Lava Falls was the most serious whitewater Buzz Holmstrom faced on the Colorado. He rowed out of the Grand Canyon onto Lake Mead and right up to Hoover Dam, fulfilled yet strangely depressed. Today's river runners who know the quality of life Buzz experienced in the canyons will understand the lines he wrote to his mother after the 1938 trip: "The last bad rapid is behind me. I had thought that once past that my reward would begin, but now everything ahead seems kind of empty, and I find I have already had my reward in the doing of the thing." But the emptiness Buzz felt at Lake Mead persisted. He served in World War II, then took a job running boats for a survey party on Oregon's Grand Ronde River. On May 18, 1946, Buzz Holmstrom borrowed a rifle and walked out of camp. They found him later a half-mile away lying face down in the sagebrush with a bullet hole in his temple. He was thirty-seven.

Norman Nevills, who pioneered commercial river running in the Grand Canyon, began taking paying passengers down the Colorado in 1938 in his specially designed cataract boats for a fee of $1000. He lined Lava on his first trip in 1938 but ran it in subsequent years. On the 1940 trip, Barry Goldwater recalled that Nevills carried food and gear around Lava on the left bank.

Then, while Goldwater waited impatiently, he deliberated for hours whether to run or line the rapid and finally elected to run down a slot on the left that, according to the annoyed Goldwater, "He must have seen the first minute he looked at the falls." The politician's impatience indicated little understanding of the boatman's psychology. Nevills, running alone, putting it all on the line, had to be sure.

The next year, 1941, Nevills was back with the first kayaker to attempt the Grand Canyon: Alexander "Zee" Grant of the Appalachian Mountain Club. His boat was a rather flimsy seventeen-foot canvas-covered craft which he had dumped in Badger, House Rock, and improbably, 164 Mile Rapid, all above Lava. Grant wanted to run the Big Drop, but after seeing it he lined his boat. Not until 1960 did Walter Kirschbaum take a kayak through Lava Falls. Today, expert kayakers relish the rapid. They frequently flip—often several times in the same run—but roll up and continue on their way. Real virtuosi can "surf" on the upstream side of Lava's huge waves and in this manner actually move upstream for short distances.

The big inflatable pontoons, the baloney boats, are at the other end of the scale of watercraft negotiating the Grand Canyon. They carry a large payload for commercial operators but have difficulty maneuvering at the critical point above Lava Falls. If they fail to straighten out by the time they reach the big hole on the right, Lava can flip the tons of rubber, metal, and people like a cork. Usually the big pontoons are simply twisted and pounded, raked by a huge volume and weight of water. But sometimes there are interesting variations. Giant "G-rigs" (three pontoons tied together) have "sandwiched" in Lava, the side units folding over upon the center one, trapping the thirty scared passengers in a rubber envelope until help arrived below the rapid to untangle the knot.

Partly as a response to the beginning of mass transport of tourists through the Grand Canyon in rubber inflatables, and partly just for fun, a few rivermen took pride in continuing the tradition of boating the Colorado in hard-hulled boats like those of Powell, Galloway, Holmstrom, and Nevills. In the 1950s, P.T.

Reilly modified the old triangle-shaped "cataract" boat for Grand Canyon whitewater, but it was a man he introduced to the river, Martin Litton, who came up with the dory idea. Litton, travel editor of *Sunset* and a director of the Sierra Club, knew that since the ancient Phoenicians and the New England cod fishers, boatmen had used sleek rowboats with flared sides and high, pointed bows and sterns to handle surf and big waves on oceans. Australian lifeguards adapted the design for surf rescues. Litton also knew that fishing guides on the McKenzie and Rogue Rivers in Oregon ran small dories. He asked the Oregon boatbuilders Keith Steele and Jerry Briggs to make him a larger version with plenty of rocker (fore-to-aft curve of the bottom) and decked interiors in which supplies could be stored in watertight hatches. In 1964 Litton and Reilly tried them out in the Grand Canyon, but the low water occasioned by the closing of the gates of Glen Canyon Dam almost left them grounded two-thirds of the way through the trip. Returning on higher water, Litton found his dories beautifully stable even in large waves. But sometimes the water gets too big for any boat. Robert Wallace, a Time-Life author, wrote about a 1971 encounter of a dory with Lava Falls:

> Litton assembled his passengers at the head of Lava Falls and made a brief speech. He would never, he said, take a boat through this stretch of water if he could avoid it. Lava Falls Rapid was a beast. I glanced at him, looking for his customary half-smile, but it was not there. Previously he had not offered his passengers a choice between riding through rapids and walking around them, but now he did. Indeed he urged them to walk, and the great majority took his advice. However, a half dozen of them remained to try the boats.
>
> I got into Litton's dory and we pushed off into quiet water above the rapids. He steered close to the right bank. Neither of us spoke; the noise of the water would have drowned our voices in any case. We entered Lava Falls at what seemed to me the perfect place and angle; but suddenly the boat plummeted headlong into a deep hole and then pitched upward at an angle of nearly 90 degrees. As the water closed over my head I had a glimpse of Litton still rowing, his oars sweeping the air. In a mo-

ment the boat righted itself; then a huge wave broke over it and tipped it so far over on its port side that it seemed certain to capsize. My head was submerged again, and when I could see daylight Litton had disappeared. The wave had swept him overboard.

The oars were still fastened in the rowlocks. I moved into Litton's place and took them, glancing hopefully left and right to find him. In a moment he bobbed up near the boat. I held out an oar and he seized it, pulling himself up to the gunwale. His bulky life jacket prevented him from climbing back into the boat, even though it was swamped and riding very low in the water; so he hung onto the gunwale as we wallowed along in the rapids. At length he said, "I'll be all right. I'll float down the river, and you try to beach the boat on the right bank."

There were two small sandy beaches on the right, separated by a half-sunken peninsula, a stoneyard of scattered rocks. On the left side of the river there was a heavy torrent of water with four- and five-foot waves: Lower Lava Falls, a continuation of the big rapids. I could scarcely move the boat, which weighed over 500 pounds empty and a ton when full of water. The current shoved it broadside against the rocks, pounded it over them, and carried it into quiet water near the second of the beaches, where I pulled it ashore and tied it to the roots of a big tamarisk. Almost 10 minutes later Litton came walking slowly up the riverbank toward me, grinning. "Pleasant day," he said.

The other wooden boats in the party also had trouble that day. People were washed from two of them, as Litton had been, while two others flipped over. Everyone, however, rode out the rapid safely and joined in towing the boats into the eddy below the falls. The only casualty was a passenger who had elected to walk around Lava Falls and sprained his ankle in the rocks.

Sometimes the margin of safety is a little thinner. Photographer Ernest Braun reports that on one hard-boat trip he watched Clyde Childress overturn with two passengers in Lava. In the aftermath, one of them could be seen swimming for shore and another head appeared in the tailwaves far downstream. But there was no sign of Childress for a minute, two minutes! Finally he struggled out onto a rock close to where the boat had flipped. The story emerged later. Instead of riding with the main flow through the rapid, Childress swam to the right to rescue a floating camera. The tricky, powerful right-side currents sucked him under and forced him into a rock tunnel. The current flowing through the tunnel pinned him firmly. Childress struggled to force his way back out, upstream. At length, his lungs bursting, he gave up, resigned to drowning. It was his salvation. His half-conscious, relaxed body popped through the downstream end of the tunnel and into the sunlight.

Such near-misses are very rare. The colorful, double-prowed boats which Martin Litton and, beginning in 1988, George Wendt operate commercially under the name Grand Canyon Dories provide one of the most safe yet exciting rides on the Colorado. Although they are now made of fiberglass, aluminum, and high-impact plastics as well as wood, the history of white-water boating rides with them down the river.

When it was still legal, motor-powered hard boats also engaged Lava Falls. In 1949 Otis "Dock" Marston pioneered downstream travel on the Colorado in motorboats. With the speed of the motors added to that of the river, his runs in Lava were more like ski jumps. Photographer Bill Belknap was with Marston on a powerboat trip in 1954. Scouting Lava, he remarked:

> Funny thing about that rapid. Each time you come to it on a river trip you wonder why you didn't have sense enough to stay home. The landscape swims before your eyes . . . a boat simply couldn't take that kind of punishment. You get down to the serious business of picking a course. The wet fact stares you in the face. There's no turning back.

Dock Marston made a beautiful run in 1954. At full throttle he roared into the right-side tongue, was clobbered, and cut left of the big wave at the bottom. Then it was Belknap's turn. As he walked to his boat he thought, "You're sure of one thing. It'll be quick. Three seconds after the first drop you'll know whether you did it right or wrong. It'd better be right. Missing the entrance by a few feet could mean disaster for men and boat."

His dual Evinrude outboards roaring, Belknap made a prac-
tice run upstream, then eased off, turned downstream in the
current, and stood up to pick his entrance:

> The current was swift and the seconds few. I picked the spot and
> leaned on the throttles with everything I had. The bow rose
> sharply and plunged down. We were in it.
>
> It seemed as though there was water over us, under us, and
> on all sides. I remembered it'd be necessary to fight left in or-
> der to avoid "the big hole." As I turned the wheel a mountain of
> water hit us from behind and both motors died. "Hang on,
> we're going in the hole!" I yelled at Willie and Jorgen, taking a
> deep breath. The bow dropped and we plunged deep under
> the big wave. Tons of water came down on us. Even clinging to
> the wheel it was hard to stay in the cockpit.
>
> Suddenly we slipped out into the air again. The cockpit was
> full. Jorgen asked, "Are we sinking?" "I don't know," I told him,
> "wait a minute and I can tell you better."

In 1960 New Zealander Jon Hamilton came to the Grand
Canyon with the propeller-less "jet" boats his family invented for
the shallow rivers of their island nation. First, the four-boat expedition made a downstream run. At Lava the driver of the lead
boat hit a standing wave so hard his boat was catapulted into the
air in a near vertical position. The resulting impact shattered his
leg, and he was flown out of the canyon by helicopter. The other
boats were more successful, and all four ultimately reached Lake
Mead. Then they turned around to attempt for the first time
running upstream through the Grand Canyon. Lava was the
rapid they most feared. Hamilton, the lead driver, made three
abortive attempts to climb it. His wife describes the next try:

> He comes at it a fourth time, faster, his white jet plume flying.
> This time he is in earnest. *The battle is on!* Right up the side he
> comes, then darts suddenly out into the rough, fighting hard,
> forcing his way diagonally across, bobbing like a tiny orange
> cork in the white water, sometimes vanishing from sight in the
> wild waves to re-appear, nose still pointing upstream, still seek-

ing a loophole in Vulcan's defenses. He has swung right across towards the north bank. Now he crabs over center again, over to the right, he has found the tongue—he's going to make it!

The boat hesitated for a moment, swaying, feeling for a hold. Then it gripped the solid water of the tongue and leapt forward, up and over the top into the smooth water beyond.

And then disaster almost struck. The motor in Hamilton's jet boat failed, and he began to slide, backwards, towards the lip of the falls. Only at the last possible moment did it catch, enabling Hamilton to crawl up and away from the rapid.

Hamilton brought the next boat almost to the base of the main falls. Then freak currents slammed it onto half-submerged rocks and he retreated. Hamilton wanted to get one more boat over the rapid before nightfall, and for forty minutes he pounded against the waves while remaining essentially in the same place. Bill Belknap, who watched the attempt from shore, observed that "Photographs can only hint at the violence of the struggle between man and river. One moment the boat teeters on a wave top. Another instant and nothing shows above the crests but the driver's head. Always the river roars and thunders, drowning every human sound."

In the morning he tried again. Joyce Hamilton watched her husband's run from the canyon rim at Toroweap, a half-mile above Lava:

> The boat looked so small and helpless as it thrashed around in the great angry river. Over and over again it was sucked down among the white waves and spewed out at the tail of the rapid. Once it came right up almost to the tongue and we waited breathlessly, and almost wept when we saw it being dragged back and back, the yellow nose leaping up as it dropped stern first into a hole.

At last Hamilton surmounted Lava, taking advantage of the surges and pauses characteristic of moving water. He literally waited for the river to relax its force for an instant; then powered ahead. With two boats up, Hamilton walked back to try the third.

Halfway up the fall he was bounced into the air by waves and landed high and dry on three protruding rocks. The Colorado raced by on all sides, but the water was shallow enough to permit men to pry the boat off with logs. Once free, Hamilton fired his engine and again soared up the tongue. The final boat failed miserably on its first attempt at Lava's tailwaves, and Hamilton beached it for a mechanical overhaul. It was almost dark when he finished, but, lights glowing, he challenged the rapid for the fourth time and won.

No one will have a chance to attempt to duplicate Hamilton's incredible feat of boatmanship. Present National Park Service regulations make motor-powered upruns of the Colorado in Grand Canyon illegal. There are good reasons, many think, to ban engines on downstream trips as well. To travel down a river is to go with the flow. It is to accept and be a part of natural processes. Upruns go against things. They symbolize man's attempt to overpower nature rather than to accept his and its limitations. The consequences of this point of view are manifest today in many of our most critical environmental problems. Conversely, going with the flow symbolizes a philosophy of harmony with the environment, the importance of which far transcends the walls of the Grand Canyon.

Lava stories are like ammo cans—every Grand Canyon river runner has one. Let two more suffice: Fred Eiseman, one of Georgie White's early boatmen, recalls a 1956 triple-rig run that underscores the wide gap between intention and reality in Lava Falls:

I'll bet Dan Davis and I studied the damn thing for two hours. We had every rock and hole spotted, and there were lots of them since the flow was only 7,400 cubic feet per second. We had our routine down pat. First pull this way. Avoid that big black one. Then that way around the hole, then a stroke and a half right past the big lateral, and so on. Well, we got into it, and it wasn't one second before we were totally out of control, ass over teakettle. We didn't flip or pancake, but we were so full of water, both externally and internally, that we couldn't take a sin-

gle stroke. Luckily the boats were so full of water that riding up
on that big black bastard at the bottom right didn't turn us over.

The next season, in June, Eiseman returned, vowing to do
better. But 1957 was a year of exceptionally high water on the
Colorado with flows varying between 90,000 and 125,000 cubic
feet per second at the time he was on the river. No one had ever
faced Lava Falls at this volume, and upstream there was much
discussion about how the rapid would look. Arriving at the normal scouting point above Lava, Eiseman and Georgie White
stared in astonishment:

> There was nothing but slick water. The entire rapids had moved
> downstream several hundred yards. Where Lava normally is,
> there was a tongue, smooth as glass from wall to wall. About
> where Lower Lava is, perhaps starting a bit upstream from it,
> there was the most god-awful collection of tailwaves that I ever
> saw in my life, making Hermit [a Grand Canyon rapid with fif-
> teen- to twenty-foot waves in normal water levels] look like a
> pup-tent. But, just down the left side of the tailwaves there was a
> nice little narrow slick spot.
>
> Georgie rode right down the middle. Discretion was surely
> our better part, and we pulled in so close to the left bank that we
> scraped all the way down. We were actually almost in an eddy,
> even at the left of the tongue, because the water in the center
> was going so fast. It seemed like an eternity before we dropped
> off on the smooth tonguelet, ran past those skyscraper tailwaves,
> and made it through without a single drop of water in the boat.

One of the most remarkable "runs" of Lava ever recorded
was the swim of Bill Beer and John Daggett. College students
casting about for a new way to spend spring vacation in 1955,
they hit upon the idea of swimming the length of the Grand
Canyon. Mae West life vests and swim fins were part of their gear,
as well as four rubber river packs that floated when sealed. No
rules and regulations got in their way; the boys just drove down
the old dirt road to Lee's Ferry and jumped in the river. With
the exception of President Harding Rapid which lacerated their

bodies, Beer and Daggett did well. On their twentieth day they came to Lava Falls. Beer describes the moment:

> The water churned, twisted and leaped into the air worse than in any rapids we had seen so far. We tossed innumerable sticks and even a log into the foaming stream, trying to find the safest course. The currents were confusing, but I finally fixed in my mind what I believed would be the best passage, and worked back upstream to where I'd left my rubber boxes.
>
> Firmly grasping the boxes, I pushed into the river and began to drift slowly toward the stormy rapids. Then the current—and I—picked up speed. I looked for the course I had mapped, but all I could see were big brown waves. Then I dropped fast and hit bottom—hard; I had gone over a four-foot waterfall. Before I could catch my breath, the stream picked me up and began rolling me over and over until I no longer knew which way was up. I just gasped for breath whenever I saw sky above. Then I was thrown high and clear by a wave and caught a glimpse of John on a rock just a few feet away. As I went under again, I braced myself to hit the rock, but another wave knocked me sideways. When I came to the surface again, the way was clear. I bounced through the rough tail of the rapids into the calm waters below and shouted triumphantly at the canyon walls.

With the exception of the IMAX actors few people since have chosen to swim Lava, but many have done so unintentionally and several have died.

It is hard to remember much about the end of a run of Lava Falls. There are the diminishing tailwaves, the overpowering sense of relief, the hugs and shouts, the endless bailing. In the exultation of the moment it is tempting to think you have conquered the rapid. Old hands know better. You never really beat the big ones. The river just decides to let you through. As you sit on the beach below Lava with a last, precious beer, stashed for days for this moment, you look back upstream at the white staircase and think, gratefully, "One more time." A related thought, if you do a lot of Big Drops, is that there are only two kinds of river runners: those who have flipped and those who are going to.

Man always kills the thing he loves, and we the pioneers have killed our wilderness. Some say we had to. Be that as it may, I am glad I shall never be young without wild country to be young in. Of what avail are forty freedoms without a blank spot on the map?

ALDO LEOPOLD

Free shackled rivers! . . .The finest fantasy of eco-warriors in the West is the destruction of [Glen Canyon] Dam and the liberation of the Colorado.

DAVE FOREMAN

HONOR ROLL

The following rapids, all of them Big Drops, have given their lives in the service of a civilization that, some feel, has yet to prove fully worthy of their sacrifice.

Lava Cliff Rapid, Grand Canyon
Colorado River, Arizona

Separation Rapid, Grand Canyon
Colorado River, Arizona

Dark Canyon Rapid, Cataract Canyon
Colorado River, Utah

Gypsum Rapids, Cataract Canyon
Colorado River, Utah

Buck Canyon Rapids, Hells Canyon
Snake River, Idaho-Oregon

Kinney Creek Rapids, Hells Canyon
Snake River, Idaho-Oregon

Squaw Creek Rapids, Hells Canyon
Snake River, Idaho-Oregon

Ashley Falls, Flaming Gorge
Green River, Utah

The Pinball
Tuolumne River, California

Celilo Falls
Columbia River, Washington

Great Falls
Missouri River, Montana

Selected Bibliography

Adney, Edwin Tappan and Howard T. Chapelle. *Bark Canoes and Skin Boats of North America.* Washington, DC: Government Printing Office, 1964.

American River Touring Association. *River Guides Manual.* Oakland, CA: ARTA, 1973.

Anderson, Fletcher and Ann Hopkinson. *Rivers of the Southwest.* Boulder, CO: Pruett, 1982.

Arighi, Scott and Margaret S. Arighi. *Wildwater Touring: A Guide to Extended Tripping By Canoe, Kayak, Drift Boat, or Raft.* New York: MacMillan, 1974.

Ashworth, William. *Hells Canyon: The Deepest Gorge on Earth.* New York: Hawthorne, 1977.

Bailey, Robert G. *Hells Canyon.* Lewiston, ID: R.G. Bailey Print Co., 1943.

————— The River of No Return. Lewiston, ID: R.G. Bailey Print Co., 1947.

Baker, Pearl. *Trail on the Water.* Boulder, CO: Pruett, 1969.

Beal, Merrill D. *Grand Canyon: The Story Behind the Scenery.* Flagstaff, AZ: KC Publications, 1967.

Beer, Bill. *We Swam the Grand Canyon.* Seattle: The Mountaineers, 1988.

Belknap, Bill and Buzz Belknap. *Canyonlands River Guide.* Boulder City, NV: Westwater Books, 1974.

Belknap, Buzz. *Grand Canyon River Guide.* Boulder City, NV: Westwater Books, 1969.

Brokaw, Tom. "That River Swallows People. Some It Gives Up; Some It Don't." *West* (Los Angeles *Times* Sunday Magazine), 1 November 1970, pp. 12-19.

Carrey, Johnny and Cort Conley. *The Middle Fork and the Sheepeater War.* Riggins, ID: Backeddy Books, 1977.

——— *River of No Return.* Cambridge, ID: Backeddy Books, 1978.

——— *Snake River of Hells Canyon.* Cambridge, ID: Backeddy Books, 1979.

Cassidy, John. *A Guide to Three Rivers: The Stanislaus, Tuolumne and South Fork of the American.* San Francisco: Friends of the River, 1981.

——— *California White Water.* San Francisco: Friends of the River, 1985.

Clark, Georgie White, and Duane Newcomb. *Georgie Clark: Thirty Years of River Running.* San Francisco: Chronicle Books, 1977.

Crampton, C. Gregory. *Land of Living Rock: The Grand Canyon and the High Plateaus.* New York: Knopf, 1972.

——— *Standing-up Country: The Canyon Lands of Utah and Arizona.* New York: Knopf, 1968.

Crumbo, Kim. *A River Runner's Guide to the History of the Grand Canyon.* Boulder, CO: Johnson Books, 1981.

Dellenbaugh, Frederick. *A Canyon Voyage: The Narrative of the Second Powell Expedition Down the Green-Colorado River from Wyoming, and the Explorations on Land in the Years 1871 and 1872.* New Haven, CT: Yale University Press, 1962.

——————— *The Romance of the Colorado River*. New York: Putnam, 1909.

DeRoss, Rose Marie. *Woman of the Rivers: Adventures of Georgie White*. Costa Mesa, CA: Gardner, 1967.

Eddy, Clyde. *Down the World's Most Dangerous River*. New York: Frederick A. Stokes Co., 1929.

Evans, Laura and Buzz Belknap. *Dinosaur River Guide*. Boulder City, NV: Westwater Books, 1973.

Goldwater, Barry. *Delightful Journey Down the Green and Colorado Rivers*. Tempe, AZ: Arizona Historical Foundation, 1970.

Hamblin, W. Kenneth and J. Keith Rigby. *Guidebook to the Colorado River: Part 1 and 2*. Provo, UT: Brigham Young University, 1968.

Hamilton, Joyce. *White Water: The Colorado River Jet Boat Expedition, 1960*. Christchurch, N.Z.: Caxton Press, 1963.

Hayes, Philip T. and George C. Simmons. *River Runners' Guide to Dinosaur National Monument and Vicinity with Emphasis on Geologic Features*. Denver: Powell Society, 1973.

Hogan, Elizabeth, ed. *Rivers of the West*. Menlo Park, CA: Lane, 1974.

Hughes, J. Donald. *The Story of Man at Grand Canyon*. Flagstaff, AZ: KC Publications, 1967.

Huser, Verne. *River Camping: Touring by Canoe, Raft, Kayak and Dory*. New York: Dial Press, 1981.

Jenkinson, Michael. *Wild Rivers of North America*. New York: Dutton, 1973.

Kolb, Ellsworth. *Through the Grand Canyon from Wyoming to Mexico.* New York: MacMillan, 1914.

Lavender, David. *River Runners of the Grand Canyon.* Tucson, AZ: University of Arizona Press, 1985.

Lee, Weston and Jeanne Lee. *Torrent in the Desert.* Flagstaff, AZ: Northland Press, 1962.

Leydet, Francois. *Time and the River Flowing: Grand Canyon.* San Francisco: Sierra Club, 1964.

Lingenfelter, R.C. *First Through the Grand Canyon.* Los Angeles: Dawson, 1958.

Litton, Martin. "The Dory Idea." *Oar and Paddle* 1 (May-June, 1974):14-18.

Martin, Charles. *Sierra Whitewater: A Paddler's Guide to the Rivers of California's Sierra Nevada.* Sunnyvale, CA: Fiddleneck Press, 1974.

McGinnis, William. *Whitewater Rafting.* New York: Quandrangle-New York Times, 1975.

Midmore, Joe. *Middle Fork History.* Reno: Harrah's Club, 1970.

Nash, Roderick, ed. *Grand Canyon of the Living Colorado.* New York: Sierra Club-Ballantine, 1970.

Nash, Roderick. *Wilderness and the American Mind.* Rev. Ed. New Haven, CT: Yale University Press, 1982.

Nash, Roderick and Robert Hackamack. "Picking Up the Pieces of the Tuolumne." *Sierra Club Bulletin* 61 (November-December 1976): 7, 8, 16.

Northwest Cartographics. *Middle Fork Salmon River: Map and Guide.* Eugene, OR: Northwest Cartographics, 1977.

Northwest Graphics. *Rogue River Canyon: River and Trail Guide.* Eugene, OR: Northwest Graphics, 1976.

Norton, Boyd. *Snake Wilderness.* San Francisco: Sierra Club, 1972.

O'Connor, Cameron and John Lazenby, eds. *First Descents: In Search of Wild Rivers.* Birmingham: Menasha Ridge Press, 1989.

Powell, John Wesley. *The Exploration of the Colorado River and Its Canyons.* New York: Dover, 1961.

Pringle, Laurence. *Wild River.* Philadelphia: Lippincott, 1972.

Quinn, James M., James W. Quinn and James G. King. *Handbook to the Rogue River Canyon.* Medford, OR: Educational Adventures, 1979.

Rabbit, Mary C. et al. *The Colorado River Region and John Wesley Powell.* Geological Survey Professional Paper 669. Washington, DC: Government Printing Office, 1969.

Schwind, Dick. *West Coast River Touring: Rogue River Canyon and South.* Beaverton, OR: Touchstone Press, 1974.

Simmons, George C. and David L. Gaskill. *River Runners' Guide to the Canyons of the Green and Colorado Rivers with Emphasis on Geological Features.* Flagstaff, AZ: Northland Press, 1969.

Smith, Dwight L. "The Engineer and the Canyon." *Utah Historical Quarterly* 28 (1960):262-273.

Stanton, Robert Brewster. *Colorado River Controversies.* Edited by James M. Chalfont. New York: Dodd, Mead, 1932.

————— *Down the Colorado.* Edited by Dwight L. Smith. Norman, OK: University of Oklahoma Press, 1965.

Staveley, Gaylord. *Broken Waters Sing: Rediscovering Two Great Rivers of the West.* Boston: Little, Brown, 1971.

Stegner, Wallace. *Beyond the Hundredth Meridian: John Wesley Powell and the Second Opening of the West.* New York: Houghton Mifflin, 1954.

Stegner, Wallace, ed. *This Is Dinosaur: Echo Park Country and Its Magic Rivers.* New York: Knopf, 1955.

Stone, Julius Frederick. *Canyon Country: The Romance of a Drop of Water and a Grain of Sand.* New York: Putnam, 1932.

Strung, Norman, Sam Curtis, and Earl Perry. *Whitewater!* New York: MacMillan, 1976.

Tejada-Flores, Lito. *Wildwater: The Sierra Club Guide to Kayaking and Whitewater Boating.* San Francisco: Sierra Club Books, 1978.

United States Forest Service. *Proceedings: River Recreation Management and Research Symposium.* General Technical Report NC-28. St. Paul, MN: North Central Forest Experiment Station, 1977.

Urban, John T. *White Water Handbook for Canoe and Kayak.* Boston: Appalachian Mountain Club, 1973.

Wallace, Robert. *The Grand Canyon.* American Wilderness Series. New York: Time-Life Books, 1972.

Waters, Frank. *The Colorado.* New York: Rinehart, 1946.

Watkins, T.H., ed. *The Grand Colorado: The Story of a River and Its Canyons.* Palo Alto, CA: American West, 1969.

Webb, Roy D. *If We Had A Boat: Green River Explorers, Adventurers and Runners.* Salt Lake City: University of Utah Press, 1986.

Whitney, Peter Dwight. *White-Water Sport: Running Rapids in Kayak and Canoe.* New York: Ronald Press Co., 1960.

Wood, Peter. *Running the Rivers of North America.* Barre, MA: Barre Publishing, 1978.

INDEX